Presented to

_____

By

_____

On the Occasion of

_____

Date

_____

THE STORY OF
JESUS

A Portrait of Christ
from the Gospels

Daniel Partner

BARBOUR
PUBLISHING, INC.
Uhrichsville, Ohio

THE STORY OF
JESUS

ISBN 1-57748-732-X

Cover Photo: Ditigal imagery ® copyright 1999 PhotoDisc, Inc.

Published by Barbour Publishing, Inc., P.O. Box 719, Uhrichsville, Ohio 44683 http://www.barbourbooks.com

Member of the
Evangelical Christian
Publishers Association

Printed in the United States of America.

DEDICATION

for John Kornblee,
my friend and brother

INTRODUCTION

The four gospels of the New Testament tell the true story of Jesus Christ. To accomplish this, each reveals the Savior in a different way: Matthew writes to first-century Jewish believers and tells of Christ the king. Mark writes to non-Jewish believers in Rome telling of Jesus the servant. Luke is addressed to a man named Theophilus (whose name means "lover of God") and shows Jesus Christ as a true human being. John speaks to a universal audience and reveals that this man is also truly God. All together, these four books compose a complete portrait of Christ.

When painting a portrait, an artist must choose the medium which will best reveal the subject. The painting may be executed on canvas or board or paper. A palette of colors and hues must be carefully mixed. Are these paints water based, oil, or acrylic? These are among the artist's many important choices—each individual element produces a desired effect in the portrait. Similarly, the authors of the Gospels, inspired by the Spirit of God, each made literary choices to make his account most effective.

In some ways the gospels are very much alike. But each tells of Jesus Christ from a different point of view. This is why the writers use different sayings, events, and timetables to tell their stories, and why their writing styles and vocabulary are not alike. Often the contrasts are very slight—like tones of one color. But the variations are often surprising. There is a purpose for this disparity: These four books, though quite different, together tell the complete story of the Savior of the world.

The Story of Jesus is a newly prepared paraphrase of Scripture based on the King James Version, which compresses the gospels into one complete chronological account. In it the reader travels from the divine conception and birth of Jesus, through his earthly ministry and agonizing death on the cross, to the triumph of his resurrection and ascension. The repetition sometimes found among the four gospels is eliminated and the rich flavor of the complete narrative is preserved. *The Story of Jesus* is not a replacement for the Scripture. Rather it is a tool that helps the reader to envision Christ's life on earth from beginning to end.

The chapters of this book correspond with the phases of Christ's life and work. Headings and subheadings, placed in the margins, outline the text and help the reader follow the flow of action. These are combined with references to the portions of the Bible from which the text is drawn, the approximate year when the events occurred, and their probable geographic location. All of this information is also gathered together in an appendix for use in further study.

Use this book to help you better know and understand who Jesus Christ is and what he has done. Because this is eternal life: to know the only true God, and Jesus Christ, whom God has sent.

Daniel Partner
Peacham, Vermont
March, 2000

CHAPTER ONE

HIS THIRTY YEARS
OF PRIVATE LIFE

To: Theophilus
Honorable sir,

Introduction

Luke 1:1-14

Many people have written orderly records of the things we believe. The disciples, who from the beginning were eyewitnesses to these things, have told them to us. From the very first, I have had a careful understanding of their accounts. So it seemed good to me to write to you about them so that you may know that the things you have learned are indeed true.

This is the record of the genealogy of Jesus Christ, the son of David, the son of Abraham:

Abraham was the father of Isaac; and Isaac was the father of Jacob; and Jacob was the father of Judah and his brothers; and Judah was the father of Perez and Zerah of Tamar; and Perez was the father of Hezron; and Hezron was the father of Ram; and Ram was the father of Amminadab; and Amminadab was the father of Nahshon; and Nahshon was the father of Salmon; and Salmon was the father of Boaz of Rahab; and Boaz was the father of Obed of Ruth; and Obed was the father of Jesse; and Jesse was the father of David the king; and David the king was the father of Solomon of her who had been the wife of Uriah;

And Solomon was the father of Rehoboam; and Rehoboam was the father of Abijah; and Abijah was the father of Asa; and Asa was the father of Jehoshaphat; and Jehoshaphat was the father of Jehoram; and Jehoram was the father of Uzziah; and Uzziah was the father of Jotham; and Jotham was the father of Ahaz; and Ahaz was the father of Hezekiah; and Hezekiah was the father of Manasseh; and Manasseh was the father of Amon; and Amon was the father of Josiah; and Josiah was the father of Jeconiah and his brothers, about the time they were carried away to Babylon:

And after they were brought to Babylon, Jeconiah was the father of Shealtiel; and Shealtiel was the father of Zerubbabel; and Zerubbabel was the father of Abiud; and Abiud was the father of Eliakim; and Eliakim was the father of Azor; and Azor was the father of Zadok; and Zadok was the father of Akim; and Akim was the father of Eliud; and Eliud was the father of Eleazar; and Eleazar was the father of Matthan; and Matthan was the father of Jacob;

And Jacob was the father of Joseph the husband of Mary, of whom was born Jesus, who is called Christ.

So all the generations from Abraham to David are fourteen generations; and from David until the carrying away into Babylon are fourteen generations; and from the carrying away into Babylon to Christ are fourteen generations.

When Jesus was about thirty years of age, he began his public ministry. He was known as the son of Joseph, who was the son of Heli, who was the son of Matthat, who was the son of Levi, who was the son of Melki, who was the son of Jannai, who was the son of Joseph, who was the son of Mattathias, who was the son of Amos, who was the son of Nahum, who was the son of Esli, who was the son of Naggai, who was the son of Maath, who was the son of Mattathias, who was the son of Semein, who was the son of Josech, who was the son of Joda;

Who was the son of Joanan, who was the son of Rhesa, who was the son of Zerubbabel, who was the son of Shealtiel, who was the son of Neri, who was the son of Melki, who was the son of Addi, who was the son of Cosam, who was the son of Elmadam, who was the son of Er, who was the son of Joshua, who was the son of Eliezer, who was the son of Jorim, who was the son of Matthat, who was the son of Levi, who was the son of Simeon, who was the son of Judah, who was the son of Joseph, who was the son of Jonam, who was the son of Eliakim, who was the son of Melea, who was the son of Menna, who was the son of Mattatha, who was the son of Nathan, who was the son of David;

Who was the son of Jesse, who was the son of Obed, who was the son of Boaz, who was the son of Salmon, who was the son of Nahshon, who was the son of Amminadab, who was the son of Ram, who was the son of Hezron, who was the son of Perez, who was the son of Judah, who was the son of Jacob, who was the son of Isaac, who was the son of Abraham, who was the son of Terah, who was the son of Nahor, who was the son of Serug, who was the son of Reu, who was the son of Peleg, who was the son of Eber, who was the son of Shelah;

Who was the son of Cainan, who was the son of Arphaxad, who was the son of Shem, who was the son of Noah, who was the son of Lamech, who was the son of Methuselah, who was the son of Enoch, who was the son of Jared, who was the son of Mahalalel, who was the son of Kenan, who was the son of Enosh, who was the son of Seth, who was the son of Adam, who was the son of God.

In the beginning was the Word, and the Word was with God, and the Word was God. The Word was in the beginning with God. Everything was made by him. Nothing that exists was made without him. Life was in him; and this life is everyone's light. The light shines in darkness; and the darkness cannot put it out.

God sent a man named John. He came to tell of the light and to help everyone believe. He himself was not the light, but he was sent to tell of the light and to report that the true light, which gives light to everyone, was going to come into the world.

The world was made by him and he was in the world, yet the world did not know him. He came to his own people, and they did not accept him. But to those who did accept and believe him, he gave the right to become the children of God. They were born of God. This was not their idea, nor did it occur out of their own passion.

So the Word became human, and lived with us. We saw his glory. It was the glory of the only Son of the Father. He was full of grace and truth. John told of him, and shouted, "This is the one I was talking about! Remember? I said that the one who is coming is much greater than I. He existed long before me."

We all received his rich blessings. They are like grace piled on top of grace. Moses gave the law; but grace and truth came through Jesus Christ. No one has ever seen God; but his only Son, who is in the Father's heart, has told us all about him.

In the time of Herod, the king of Judea, there was a priest of the order of Abijah named Zechariah. His wife, Elizabeth, was related to the first priest, Aaron. They both righteously obeyed God's commandments and followed the Jewish customs. But they were very old and had no children, because Elizabeth was unable to conceive.

It so happened that when it was Zechariah's turn to do the duty of a priest before God. He was chosen by lot (as was the custom) to burn incense in the temple of the Lord. At the time he was burning the incense, a crowd of people were outside, praying. And an angel of the Lord

His Birth

John's Birth
Is Promised
in Jerusalem
c. 7 B.C.

Luke 1:5-25

appeared to him, standing on the right side of the incense altar. When Zechariah saw the angel he was full of fear.

But the angel said to him, "Don't be afraid, Zechariah. Your prayer has been heard. Your wife Elizabeth will give birth to a son, and you will name him John. Not only will you have true joy and gladness, but many people will rejoice about the birth of this boy, because the Lord will consider him to be a great man. He will not drink wine or strong drink; he will be filled with the Holy Spirit from the moment of his birth, and he will bring many Israelites back to their God. He will go ahead of the coming Lord with the spirit and power of Elijah, and prepare the people for Christ's appearance. He will turn the hearts of fathers to love their children, and change disobedient people so they can understand righteous wisdom."

Zechariah said to the angel, "How do I know this is true? After all, I'm an old man, and my wife is well along in years." The angel answered, "I am Gabriel. I stand in the presence of God and have been sent to speak to you and tell you this good news. Because you do not believe me, you will be unable to speak until the very day that these things happen. And they will happen in due time."

The people outside were waiting for Zechariah, and were amazed that he stayed in the temple so long. When he came out, he could not speak to them. He used hand signals and they figured out that he had seen a vision in the temple. But he remained speechless.

As soon as his required service was done, Zechariah went home. Shortly after, his wife Elizabeth became pregnant. She withdrew into seclusion for five months. "The Lord has taken away my disgrace!" she said. "He has been so kind to me."

Six months after Elizabeth became pregnant, God sent the angel Gabriel to a town in Galilee called Nazareth. There lived a young woman who was engaged to marry a man named Joseph, a descendant of David, the king of Israel. This woman's name was Mary.

The angel came to her and said, "Greetings, the Lord is with you. You are

Gabriel Visits Mary
in Nazareth
c. 6 B.C.

Luke 1:26-38

the most blessed of all women." When she saw him, she was troubled by what he said and wondered what he meant.

The angel said, "Don't be afraid, Mary. God has blessed you. You will become pregnant, give birth to a son, and give him the name Jesus. He will be great, and will be called the Son of the Highest. The Lord God will give him the throne of his forefather David, and he will rule over Israel forever. His kingdom will never end."

Then Mary said to the angel, "How can this be? I've never been with a man."

The angel answered, "The Holy Spirit will come upon you, and the power of the Highest will overshadow you. Therefore the holy one you will bring to birth will be called the Son of God. Look at your cousin Elizabeth, who was once unable to conceive; but now, in her old age, she is pregnant with a son. This is the sixth month of her pregnancy. So nothing is impossible with God."

Mary said, "I am the Lord's servant. Let it be just as you have said." Then the angel departed.

Mary arose and hurried to a town in the hill country of Judah, to the house of Zechariah. She entered the house and greeted Elizabeth. At the moment when Elizabeth heard Mary's greeting, her baby leaped within her and Elizabeth was filled with the Holy Spirit. She spoke with a loud voice, saying, "You are more blessed than all women. And your child is blessed as well. Why would the mother of my Lord come to visit me? For as soon as I heard the sound of your greeting, my baby leaped for joy in my womb. You believed and you are blessed—the things the Lord has told you will happen."

Mary said, "My soul exalts the Lord, and my spirit rejoices in God my Savior, for he has seen the humble state of his servant. From now on, all generations will call me blessed. The mighty one has done great things for me. His name is holy and his mercy is upon people in every generation who fear him. He has used his strong arm to scatter those who are proud and arrogant. He has put down the powerful, and raised up the lowly. He has fed the hungry with good things; and the rich he has sent away empty. He has helped his servant Israel, remembering his promise of eternal mercy to our ancestors—Abraham and his children."

Mary stayed with Elizabeth about three months, before returning to her own house.

John is Born in the Judean Hills

Luke 1:57-80

When the time came for Elizabeth to deliver her child, she gave birth to a son. Her neighbors and relatives heard how the Lord had been merciful to her, and they rejoiced with her. When on the eighth day they came to circumcise the child, they wanted to name him Zechariah, after his father. But his mother said, "No. He will be called John."

They said to her, "No one in your family is named John." So they made signs to his father, asking what he wanted to call the boy. He motioned for a writing tablet, and wrote, "His name is John." They all marveled. Immediately Zechariah could speak again and he praised God.

Everyone living nearby was awestruck by these events, and the story was told around the hill country of Judea. Those who heard, remembered, and wondered, "What kind of child will this be?" They declared, "The Lord is with him."

Zechariah was filled with the Holy Spirit and spoke this prophecy: "Bless the Lord God of Israel! He has come to his people and redeemed them; he has raised up a horn of salvation for us in the royal house of his servant David, just as he promised through his holy prophets from the beginning. We will be saved from our enemies, and from all those who hate us. God has remembered the holy covenant and will be merciful, as promised to our ancestors in the oath he swore to our father Abraham. We have been rescued from our enemies so that we can serve God all the days of our lives in holiness and righteousness without fear.

"You, my son, will be the prophet of the Highest; and you will go ahead of the Lord to prepare the way for him to come. You will bring to God's people the knowledge of salvation through his forgiveness of their sins. This is the tender mercy of our God: The dayspring from above has visited us to give light to the people who sit in darkness and in the shadow of death, to guide our feet into the way of peace."

And the child grew, and became strong in spirit. Eventually, he lived alone in the desert until the day he began do God's work in Israel.

An Angel
Visits Joseph
in Nazareth

Matt. 1:18-25

The birth of Jesus Christ happened like this: His mother Mary was engaged to marry Joseph. But before they came together, she was made pregnant by the Holy Spirit.

Now Joseph was an honest, righteous man. He didn't want to bring Mary to public shame, so he thought he should quietly break their engagement. But while he thought about this, the angel of the Lord appeared to him in a dream and said, "Joseph, son of David, don't be afraid to take Mary as your wife. The child in her womb has been conceived by the Holy Spirit. She will give birth to a son, and you will call him Jesus, because he will save his people from their sins."

All this happened to fulfill the words spoken by the Lord through the prophet:

"Look, a virgin will become pregnant, and will give birth to a son. They will call his name Immanuel, which means, 'God with us.'"

Then Joseph woke up from his sleep and did what the angel had told him. He took Mary as his wife and they did not share the marriage bed until she gave birth to her firstborn son, whom he named Jesus.

At that time, Caesar Augustus commanded that a census should be taken in the Roman Empire. (This happened when Cyrenius was governor of Syria.) So all returned to their hometown to register for the census. Joseph and Mary (who was quite pregnant by this time) went up from Nazareth in Galilee to Bethlehem in Judea, the ancient home of Joseph's ancestor David, to be counted in the census. While they were there, Mary went into labor. She gave birth to her firstborn son, carefully wrapped him in blankets, and laid him in a feed trough. (There was no room for them in the inn.)

He is Born
in Bethlehem
c. 6 B.C.

Luke 2:1-7

Angels
Visit the
Shepherds
near
Bethlehem

Luke 2:8-20

That night, in a field near Bethlehem, shepherds were watching over their flock. The angel of the Lord came to them, and the shining glory of the Lord surrounded them—and they were very afraid.

The angel said to them, "Don't be afraid. Look, I bring you good news of great joy for all people. Today the Savior has been born in David's town, Bethlehem. It is Christ the Lord!

"Here is how you will know him: look for the baby wrapped in blankets and lying in a feed trough." Suddenly there was with the angel a multitude of the heavenly host, praising God and saying, "Glory to God in the highest, and on earth peace, goodwill toward men."

When the angels went away into heaven, the shepherds said to each other, "Let's go to Bethlehem, and see this thing which the Lord has told us."

They hurried and found Mary and Joseph, and the baby lying in a feed trough. When they saw them, the shepherds went out and told everyone about what had happened. And those who heard were amazed over what the shepherds said. But Mary kept all these things in her memory and often pondered them. The shepherds returned to their flocks, glorifying and praising God for all the things they had heard and seen.

After eight days, it was time to circumcise the child. He was named Jesus, the name given to him by the angel before he was conceived.

His Early Life

He Is Circumcised *in Bethlehem*

Luke 2:21

Then the time came for the purification offering required by the law of Moses. So they brought Jesus to Jerusalem to present him to God, because the law of the Lord says, "Every firstborn boy will be given to the Lord." There they offered a sacrifice in keeping with the law of the Lord: "Offer either a pair of turtledoves, or two young pigeons."

He Is Presented to God *in Jerusalem*

Luke 2:22-39

There was a man in Jerusalem named Simeon. He was righteous and devout and was waiting for the Messiah to rescue Israel. The Holy Spirit was upon him, and revealed to him that he would not die before he had seen the Lord's Messiah. At the same time that Jesus' parents brought the child to do what the law required of them, Simeon was led by the Spirit into the temple. He took Jesus in his arms, praised God, and said, "Lord, now your servant can die in peace, just as you promised. For I have seen your salvation, the Messiah whom you have given to all people. He is light for the Gentiles, and the glory of your people Israel." Joseph and Mary marveled at the things that were said about Jesus. Simeon blessed them all, and said to Mary, Jesus' mother, "Look! This child will cause many in Israel to fall and rise again. He will be a sign to them and will be rejected. The thoughts of many hearts will be revealed; and yes, a sword will pierce through your own soul."

Anna, a prophet (the daughter of Phanuel, of the tribe of Asher), was there at the time. She had been married seven years when her husband died (she was now about eighty-four years old). Anna never left the temple, but served God, fasting and praying night and day. She came upon them, gave thanks to the Lord, and spoke of Jesus to all those nearby— people who were waiting for a king to come and rescue Jerusalem.

When Joseph and Mary had done all the things required of them by the law, they returned to their town, Nazareth of Galilee.

Herod was the king when Jesus was born in Bethlehem of Judea. At that time, wise men came from the east to Jerusalem. There they inquired: "Where is the new-born king of the Jews? We have seen his star from our homes in the east, and have come here to worship him."

When Herod heard about this, he was worried, as was all of Jerusalem. So he gathered all the leading Jewish priests and scholars together and demanded they tell him where this Christ would be born. They told him: "In Bethlehem of Judea, for the prophet has written, 'And you Bethlehem, in the land of Judah, are not the least among the princes of Judah: for out of you will come a governor, who will rule my people Israel.'"

Herod privately called the wise men and carefully inquired as to when the star had appeared. Then he sent them to

The Wise Men Arrive *in Jerusalem and Bethlehem* c. 4 B.C.

Matt. 2:1-12

Bethlehem, and said, "Go and search for the young child. When you have found him, bring me word. I want to worship him too." After they had spoken to the king, the wise men departed from Jerusalem, and the star which they had first seen from their homes in the east went ahead of them, until it stopped over the place where the child was.

When they saw the star, they rejoiced with great joy. They came into the house, and when they saw the child with Mary his mother, they fell down, and worshipped him. When they opened their treasures, they presented to him gifts of gold, frankincense, and myrrh. But being warned by God in a dream that they should not return to Herod, they departed into their own country by another way.

He Escapes
to Egypt
from Nazareth

Matt. 2:13-18

After the wise men departed, the angel of the Lord appeared to Joseph in a dream, and said, "Get up, take the young child and his mother, flee into Egypt, and stay there until I bring you word. Herod is going to try to kill the child."

Joseph got up that night, took the

child and his mother, and left for Egypt. They stayed there until Herod died. This fulfilled the Lord's words spoken through the prophet: "I have called my son out of Egypt."

When Herod saw that he had been ignored by the wise men, he was enraged, and sent soldiers to kill all the children two years old and under, in Bethlehem and the nearby towns. This fulfilled the prophecy of Jeremiah, who said, "In Rama there was heard a voice of lamentation, weeping, and great mourning. It was Rachel weeping for her children, and she would not be comforted, because they were gone."

When Herod died, an angel of the Lord appeared to Joseph in a dream and said, "Get up and take the young child and his mother out of Egypt, and go into the land of Israel. The man who sought to take the boy's life is dead."

Joseph got up, took the child and his mother, and returned to Israel. But when he heard that Archelaus was reigning in Judea in place of his father Herod, he was

He Returns
from Egypt
to Nazareth

Matt. 2:19-23
Luke 2:40

afraid to go there. So, having been warned by God in a dream, he detoured to Galilee, and made his home in a town called Nazareth. This happened to fulfill the prediction of the prophets: "He will be called a Nazarene."

And the child grew to be strong in spirit and filled with wisdom. The grace of God was with him.

He Visits
Jerusalem
C. A.D. 9

Luke 2:41-50

Jesus' parents went to Jerusalem every year for the feast of the Passover. So when he was twelve years old, they went up to Jerusalem for the feast. When the feast was over, the family returned home, but Jesus stayed behind in Jerusalem. Joseph and his mother did not know that he had stayed behind. They thought he was among the group they were traveling with. His parents went a day's journey while they looked for him among their relatives and friends. When they did not find him, they went back to Jerusalem to look for him.

After searching for three days, they found him in the temple, sitting among the teachers, listening and asking questions.

Everyone that heard him was astonished at his understanding, and at the way he could answer the teachers' questions. When his parents found him, they were amazed. His mother said to him, "Son, why have you done this? Look, your father and I have been so worried as we looked for you." He answered, "Why did you look for me? Don't you know that I must do my Father's business?" But they did not understand what he meant.

He Grows to Manhood *in Nazareth*

Luke 2:51-52

Jesus went down from Jerusalem with them, came to Nazareth, and obeyed them. But his mother remembered all these things. And Jesus grew in maturity and in wisdom, and was loved by God and the people.

CHAPTER TWO

THE BEGINNING OF THE GOSPEL

In the fifteenth year of the reign of Tiberius Caesar, Pontius Pilate was governor of Judea, and Herod was tetrarch of Galilee. His brother Philip was tetrarch of Iturea and of the region of Traconitis, Lysanias was the tetrarch of Abilene, and Annas and Caiaphas were the high priests.

At that time, God's instructions came to John, the son of Zechariah, in the wilderness and he came out into the country around the Jordan River. There he preached the baptism of repentance for the forgiveness of sins, saying, "Repent, for the

Groundwork for Christ's Ministry

John Prepares the Way
in Judea
c. A.D. 27

Matt. 3:1-12
Mark 1:1-8
Luke 3:1-18

kingdom of heaven is almost here."

This happened just as it is written in the book of Isaiah the prophet, "One voice is crying in the wilderness, 'Prepare the way of the Lord, make his paths straight.' Every valley will be filled in, and every mountain and hill will be flattened. The crooked road will be made straight, and the rough ways will be made smooth. All of humanity will see the salvation of God."

John's clothing was made of camel's hair, and he wore a leather belt around his waist. His food was locusts and wild honey. The people of Jerusalem, and Judea, and all the region around the Jordan went out to see him. They confessed their sins, and he baptized them in the Jordan River.

Then he said to the crowd that came to be baptized, "O generation of snakes! Who has warned you to flee from the coming wrath? Produce fruit in your lives to prove you have repented. Do not simply say, 'Abraham is our father.' Listen to me: God is able to bring forth children for Abraham out of these stones. And now the ax has cut to the root of the trees. Every tree which does not produce good fruit is cut down and thrown into the fire."

The people asked him, "What should we do?" He answered, "If you have two coats, give one to a person who has none. If you have food, do the same." Then tax collectors came to be baptized, and said, "Master, what should we do?" He said, "Collect no more tax than you should." And soldiers demanded, "What should we do?" He said to them, "Don't hurt anyone, or lie about anyone, and be content with your wages."

The people were excited and everyone wondered whether John was the Messiah. So John answered them all, "I baptize you in water. But a stronger man is coming. I am not worthy to untie the lace of his shoe. He will baptize you with the Holy Spirit and with fire. A threshing fan is in his hand, and he will thoroughly clean the chaff from his threshing floor and gather the wheat into his barn. But he will burn the chaff with relentless fire." And John preached many other things to the people.

John
Baptizes
Jesus
*in the
Jordan River*

*Matt. 3:13-17
Mark 1:9-11
Luke 3:21-23*

When all the people were baptized, Jesus came from Galilee to Jordan to be baptized by John. But John refused. "I need to be baptized by you," he said, "and you come to me?" Jesus said to him, "Do it anyway. It is good for us to do what is right." Then John baptized him.

When Jesus came up out of the water, the heavens opened to him and he saw the Spirit of God coming down like a dove, and it landed on him. Then a voice from heaven said, "This is my Son. I love him and he pleases me." At that time Jesus was about thirty years of age.

The Devil
Entices Jesus
in Judea

*Matt. 4:1-11
Mark 1:12-13
Luke 4:1-13*

Full of the Holy Spirit, Jesus returned from the Jordan and was led by the Spirit into the wilderness. There he was enticed by the devil for forty days. He fasted forty days and forty nights, and afterward he was hungry.

The devil said to him, "If you are the Son of God, command that this stone be made bread." Jesus answered him, "It is written, 'Man will not live by bread alone, but by every word that proceeds out of the mouth of God.' "

The devil took him up into a high mountain, quickly showed him all the kingdoms of the world, and said, "I will give all this power and all this glory to you. After all, it belongs to me. I can give it to anyone I want. If you will worship me, it will all be yours." Jesus answered him, "Get back, Satan. You know that it is written in Scripture, 'You will worship the Lord your God, and will only serve him.'"

The devil brought him to Jerusalem, to a high tower in the temple, and said, "If you are the Son of God, jump down from here. You know that it is written in Scripture, 'He will put his angels in charge of your safety. They will hold you with their own hands so you will not even trip on a stone.'" Jesus said to him, "It has been said, 'You will not tempt the Lord your God.'" Then the devil ended his temptation, and departed from him for a while. And angels came and ministered to Jesus.

The religious leaders in Jerusalem sent priests and Levites to John to ask, "Who

John's Account of Jesus *in Bethabara*

John 1:19-34

are you?" This is what John said: "I am not the Christ."

So they asked him, "Are you Elijah?" He said, "I am not."

"Are you the prophet?" He answered, "No."

Then they asked, "Who are you? We have to give an answer to the men who sent us. What do you have to say about yourself?"

John said, "I am the voice of one crying in the wilderness, 'Make straight the way of the Lord,' just as the prophet Isaiah said."

These Pharisees asked him, "Why do you baptize then, if you are not Christ, or Elijah, or the prophet?" John answered, "I baptize with water. But there is a man among you, whom you do not know. He is coming after me but has been chosen before me. I am not even worthy to untie his shoelace." This happened in Bethany, beyond the Jordan, where John was baptizing.

The next day, John saw Jesus coming to him and said "Look, the Lamb of God, who takes away the sin of the world! This is the man I was talking about when I said, 'A man is coming after me who was chosen before me; because he was before me.' I did not know him. But I baptized with water so that Israel could know him."

Then John said, "I saw the Spirit coming from heaven like a dove, and it landed on him. I did not know him. But God, who sent me to baptize with water, said to me, 'The man upon whom the Spirit lands, that is the one who baptizes with the Holy Spirit.' And I saw this. So I tell you that this is the Son of God."

The next day, John and two of his disciples watched Jesus as he walked by, and John said, "Look, the Lamb of God!" The two disciples heard this, and followed Jesus.

Jesus turned, saw them following, and said to them, "What do you want?" They said, "Rabbi (which means teacher), where do you live?"

He said, "Come and see." They came and saw where he lived, and stayed with him that day, because it was about four

He Gathers
Disciples

• By the River
at the Jordan

John 1:35-42

o'clock in the afternoon. One of these two was Andrew, Simon Peter's brother.

He found his brother, Simon, and said to him, "We have found the Messiah." Andrew brought Simon to Jesus. When Jesus saw Simon, he said, "You are Simon the son of John. You will be called Cephas" (which translates to Peter).

• By the Lake at the Sea of Galilee

Matt. 4:18-22
Mark 1:16-20
Luke 5:1-11
John 1:43-51

The following day, Jesus went to Galilee. As he was walking by the Sea of Galilee, he saw two brothers, Simon, who was called Peter, and Andrew his brother. They were casting a net into the lake, because they were fishermen. And he said to them, "Follow me, and I will make you fishers of men." And right away they left their nets and followed him.

Going on from there, he saw two other brothers, James the son of Zebedee, and John his brother, in a boat with Zebedee, mending their nets. He called them. They immediately left the boat and their father with the hired servants, and followed him.

Next he found Philip, and said, "Follow me." Now Philip was from Bethsaida, the town of Andrew and Peter. Then Philip found Nathanael, and said to him, "We have found the man about whom Moses and the prophets wrote—Jesus of Nazareth, the son of Joseph." Nathanael said, "Can anything good come out of Nazareth?" Philip said, "Come and see."

Jesus saw Nathanael coming and said, "Look, an Israelite in whom is no dishonesty!" Nathanael said to him, "How do you know me?" Jesus answered, "I saw you under the fig tree before Philip talked to you." Nathanael answered, "Rabbi, you are the Son of God; you are the King of Israel!"

Jesus said to him, "Just because I said, 'I saw you under the fig tree,' is that why you believe? You will see greater things than these." And then he said, "Here is the truth: You will see heaven open and the angels of God going up and down on the Son of Man like a ladder."

As Jesus stood by the lake of Gennesaret, the people squeezed around him to hear the word of God. There were two boats moored in the lake. The fishermen had left them and were washing their nets.

Jesus boarded one of the boats, which was Simon's, and asked him to set out a little from the land. He sat down and taught the people out of the boat.

When he finished speaking, Jesus said to Simon, "Launch out into the deep water, and let down your nets." Simon said to him, "Master, we have worked all night and have caught nothing. But because you say so, I will let down the net." When the fishermen did this, they netted many, many fish, and their net broke. So they called to their partners in the other boat to come and help them. They came, and filled both the boats with fish, so that they began to sink.

When Simon Peter saw this, he fell down at Jesus' knees, saying, "Depart from me; I am a sinful man, O Lord." He and the other fishermen, including James and John, the sons of Zebedee, who were partners with Simon, were astonished at the number of fish they had caught. Jesus said to Simon, "Don't be afraid; from now on you will catch people." They brought their boats to land, left everything, and followed him.

Three days later, there was a marriage in Cana of Galilee. Jesus' mother was there and Jesus and his disciples were invited to the wedding as well. When the people wanted wine, Jesus' mother said to him, "They have no wine." Jesus said to her, "Woman, that is not my concern. It is not yet time for me to do such things." His mother said to the servants, "Do whatever he says."

There were six stone jars there for use in the Jewish ceremonies. Each held twenty or thirty gallons. Jesus said to the servants, "Fill the jars with water." They filled them up to the brim. He said to them, "Draw the liquid out of one jar and give it to the host of the feast." And they did it. When the host tasted the water that was made into wine, he did not know where it came from (but the servants who drew the water knew). The host of the feast called the bridegroom and said to him, "Every man serves good wine at the beginning—then he serves the cheap wine. But you have kept the good wine until now."

Jesus did this miraculous sign in Cana

of Galilee. In this way, he exhibited his glory, and his disciples believed in him. After this, he went down to Capernaum with his mother, his brothers, and his disciples. They stayed there for a few days.

His Early Work

Purifying the Temple
in Jerusalem
C. A.D. 28

John 2:13-22

The time of the Passover arrived, and Jesus went up to Jerusalem. In the temple, he found money changers and people who sold oxen and sheep and doves for sacrifices. He made a whip out of small cords and ran them all out of the temple, along with their sheep and oxen. He spilled the changers' money, and overthrew the tables. Then he said to the people selling doves, "Take these things out of here. Don't make my Father's house a house of merchandise."

Then his disciples remembered that it is written in the Scriptures, "My zeal for your house has consumed me."

But the Jewish leaders said to him, "Since you do these things, show us a miracle." Jesus said to them, "Destroy this temple, and in three days I will raise it up."

Then the Jews said, "It took forty-six

years to build this temple. Will you build it in three days?" But he was speaking of the temple of his body. When he arose from the dead, his disciples remembered that he had said this to them; and they believed the Scripture and the word which Jesus had spoken.

When he was in Jerusalem for the Passover, many people believed in him when they saw the miracles he did. But Jesus did not trust them, because he understood people and did not need anyone to tell him about human nature. He knew what is in humanity.

Declaring the New Birth *in Jerusalem*

John 2:23-3:21

But there was a Pharisee named Nicodemus, a Jewish leader, who came to Jesus by night and said to him, "Rabbi, we know that you are a teacher sent from God. No one could do the miracles you do, unless God is with him." Jesus said to him, "I'll tell you the truth, unless a man is born again, he cannot see the kingdom of God."

Nicodemus said, "How can a man be born when he has grown old? Can he enter into his mother's womb a second time and be born?"

Jesus answered, "I'll tell you the truth, a man has to be born of water and of the Spirit. If not, he cannot enter into the kingdom of God. Whoever is born of the flesh is flesh; and whoever is born of the Spirit is spirit. Do not marvel. Yes, I said, 'You must be born again.' Yet, the wind blows and you hear the sound but cannot tell where it comes from and where it goes. So it is with everyone who is born of the Spirit."

Nicodemus said, "How can these things be?"

Jesus answered, "Are you a teacher of Israel and yet do not know about this? Here is the truth: I speak about what I know, and testify of what I have seen. But you Jewish leaders will not accept what I say. I have told you about things that happen on earth and you do not believe. How will you believe if I tell you about heavenly things? The only man who has ascended up to heaven, is the one that came down from heaven. That is: the Son of Man who is in heaven.

"Do you remember how Moses lifted

up the serpent in the wilderness? In the same way, the Son of Man will be lifted up on a cross so that whoever believes in him will not perish, but have eternal life. This will happen because God loved the world so much that he gave it his only Son, so that whoever believes in him will not perish, but will have eternal life.

"God did not send the Son into the world to condemn the world. The Son came so that the world could be saved through him. Whoever believes in him will not be condemned. But whoever does not believe is condemned already, because he has not believed in the name of the only Son of God.

"This is the condemnation: Light has come into the world, but people loved darkness rather than light. Why? Because they do evil things. All who do evil hate the light and do not come to the light, because, in it, their sins will be exposed. But whoever lives the truth comes to the light, so it can be seen that his deeds are accepted by God."

John
Concludes
His Ministry
in Aenon

Luke 3:19-20
John 3:22-36

After this, Jesus and his disciples came into Judea. There he stayed and baptized people. John had not yet been imprisoned, so he was baptizing in Aenon near Salim, where there was plenty of water. People came to him and were baptized.

Then some of John's disciples and the Jewish leaders were discussing the problem of purification of the body. So they came to John and said, "Rabbi, remember the man who was with you by the Jordan River, the one you told us about? Look, he is baptizing nearby, and everyone is going to him instead of us."

John said, "A person has nothing unless it is given to him from heaven. You know that I said, 'I am not the Christ.' I have been sent ahead of him. The one with the bride is the bridegroom. The friend of the bridegroom, who stands by and listens, rejoices because he can hear the bridegroom's voice. So I am joyfully satisfied with this.

"He must increase, and I must decrease. The one who comes from above is above all. The one who is of the earth is earthly, and speaks of the earth. The one who comes from heaven is above all, and tells of what he has seen and heard, yet no one accepts what he says. I have received his testimony, and swear that God is true. For the man whom God has sent to us speaks God's words and has God's unlimited Spirit upon him. The Father loves the Son, and has given everything to him. Whoever believes in the Son has eternal life. Whoever does not believe in the Son will not see eternal life. Instead, he will know the wrath of God."

Then Herod the tetrarch imprisoned John, because John had condemned Herod for marrying his brother Philip's wife, Herodias (and for all the other evil Herod had done).

The Lord heard that the Pharisees knew that he baptized more disciples than John (though Jesus himself did not baptize, his disciples did). Jesus also learned that John had been imprisoned. So he left Judea, and went to Galilee. To get there, he had to go through Samaria.

There he came to a town called Sychar, near the parcel of land that Jacob gave to

The Water at Jacob's Well *in Samaria*

Matt. 4:12
John 4:1-26

his son Joseph. Jacob's well was there. At about noon, Jesus was weary from travel and sat near the well. His disciples had gone away to the town to buy food. Just then, a Samaritan woman came to the well to draw water. Jesus said to her, "Give me some water to drink, please."

The woman said to him, "How is it that you, a Jew, ask me for a drink? I am only a woman from Samaria." (The Jews have no dealings with the Samaritans.)

Jesus answered, "If you knew the gift of God, and who is saying to you, 'Give me a drink,' you would have asked me the same thing, and I would have given you living water."

The woman said to him, "Sir, you have nothing with which to draw out the water, and the well is deep. Where will you get that living water? Are you greater than our father Jacob, who gave us this well? He drank here himself, so did his children, and his cattle."

Jesus said to her, "Whoever drinks the water from this well will thirst again. But whoever drinks the water that I will give, will never thirst. Instead, my water will be in him like a living well of water springing up into eternal life."

The woman said, "Sir, give me this water so that I will not thirst and have to come here every day to get water."

Jesus answered her, "Go, call your husband, and come back."

The woman said, "I have no husband."

Jesus said, "That's right. You said, 'I have no husband,' because you have had five husbands; and the man you're living with now is not your husband. So you spoke the truth."

The woman said to him, "Sir, I see that you are a prophet. Our fathers worshipped at this mountain; and you Jews say that Jerusalem is the place where people should worship."

Jesus said to her, "Woman, believe me, the time is coming when you will neither worship the Father at this mountain, nor at Jerusalem. In fact, you Samaritans do not even know what you worship. We Jews, on the other hand, do know whom we worship. Salvation is of the Jews. But the time has come when true worshippers will worship the Father in spirit and in truth, because the Father is looking for people to worship him in this way. God is Spirit, and those who worship him must worship him in spirit and in truth."

The woman said to him, "I know that the Messiah is coming. He is called Christ and when he comes he will tell us all things."

Jesus said to her, "I am he."

The Gospel
in Sychar

John 4:27-44

Just then, his disciples came back from town. They were amazed that Jesus was talking with a woman, yet no one said, "What do you want?" or "Why are you talking with her?"

The woman then left her water pot, went into the town, and said to the people there, "Come, see a man who told me everything I ever did. This must be the Christ!" So they all came to him.

Meanwhile his disciples said, "Master, eat some food."

But he said, "I have food that you know nothing about."

The disciples said to each another, "Has anyone brought him something to eat?" Jesus told them, "My food is to do the will of the one who sent me, and to finish his work. Do not say, 'There are still four months before harvest.' Open your eyes and look at the fields; they are ready to harvest. Whoever reaps the harvest will get paid and will gather the crops of eternal life. So both the one who sows and the one who reaps can rejoice together. The saying is true: 'One sows, and another reaps.' I sent you to reap what you did not work for. Other people labored, and you have benefited from their work."

Many Samaritans in the town believed in him because the woman declared, "He told me everything that I ever did." When the Samaritans came to Jesus, they begged him to stay with them. So he stayed there two days and many more believed because of his words. They said to the woman, "Now we believe, not because of what you say, but we have heard him ourselves and know that this indeed is the Christ, the Savior of the world."

After two days, he left and went to Galilee; for Jesus himself testified that a prophet has no honor in his own country.

Chapter Three

His Work in Galilee Begins

He returned in the authority of the Spirit to Galilee, preaching the gospel of the kingdom of God, and saying, "The time has come, the kingdom of God is here: Repent and believe the gospel." When he came to Galilee, the Galileans welcomed him, because they had seen all that he did in Jerusalem at the feast. He was famous throughout the region, taught in their synagogues, and was glorified by everyone.

Jesus left Nazareth and went to live in Capernaum, which is on the lakeshore

Returning with Authority to Galilee

Matt. 4:12-17
Mark 1:14-15
Luke 4:14-15
John 4:45

near Zebulun and Naphtali. He taught there on the Sabbath. This fulfilled the words of Isaiah the prophet, who said, "The land of Zebulun, and the land of Naphtali, by the way of the sea, beyond Jordan, Galilee of the Gentiles; the people who sat in darkness saw great light, and to them who sat in the region and shadow of death, light is sprung up."

From that time, Jesus began to preach, "Repent: for the kingdom of heaven is here." The people were astonished at his teaching, because his words had authority.

Healing with His Words
in Cana

John 4:46-54

Jesus went again to Cana of Galilee, where he had made the water into wine. A nobleman at Capernaum, whose son was sick, heard that Jesus had come to Galilee. He went to Jesus and asked him to come and heal his son (who was at the point of death).

Jesus said to him, "Unless you see signs and wonders, you will not believe in me." The nobleman said to him, "Sir, come or my child will die." Jesus said, "Go on your way; your son is alive." The man believed what Jesus said to him, and went his way.

As he was going down to his house, his servants met him and told him, "Your son is alive."

He asked them the time the boy began to revive. They said, "The fever left him yesterday at one o'clock in the afternoon." So the father knew that it had happened at the same time Jesus had said to him, "Your son is alive." And he believed, and his whole household believed as well. This is the second miraculous sign that Jesus did when he came out of Judea into Galilee.

Jesus went to Nazareth, where he had been raised. As was his custom, he went into the synagogue on the Sabbath day and stood up to read. They handed him the book of the prophet Isaiah. He opened the book and found the place where it was written, "The Spirit of the Lord is upon me, because he has anointed me to preach the gospel to the poor; he has sent me to heal the brokenhearted, to preach deliverance to the captives, and recovery of sight to the blind; to set at liberty those who are bruised; to preach the acceptable year of the Lord." He closed the book, gave it to

Rejected in His Hometown
in Nazareth

Luke 4:16-30

the minister, and sat down. The eyes of all in the synagogue were upon him. He said to them, "Today, this Scripture is fulfilled."

Everyone saw this and wondered at his gracious words. They said, "Isn't this Joseph's son?" He said to them, "You will no doubt quote this proverb: 'Physician, heal yourself. Whatever we have heard that you have done in Capernaum, do here in your country also.' So it is true, no prophet is accepted in his own country. But I tell you the truth, many widows were in Israel in the days of Elijah when there was no rain for three years and six months, causing a serious famine in the land. But Elijah was not sent to them. Instead he went to Zarephath, a town in Sidon, to a woman there who was a widow. And there were many lepers in Israel in the time of Elisha the prophet; and none of them was cleansed except Naaman the Syrian."

Everyone in the synagogue heard these things and was very angry. They stood up and drove him out of the town to the edge of the hill where their town was built, so that they could throw him over the edge.

But he walked through the crowd and went on his way.

He traveled down to Capernaum, and taught them on the Sabbath days. They were amazed at his teaching because his words had authority.

In the synagogue, there was a man who had a spirit of an unclean devil. It cried out with a loud voice, "Let us alone; what have we to do with you, Jesus of Nazareth? Have you come to destroy us? I know who you are—the Holy One of God." And Jesus rebuked him, "Be quiet and come out of him." When the devil had thrown the man down, and cried with a loud voice, he came out of him, and did not hurt him. Everyone was amazed, and said to each other, "What a word is this! He commands the unclean spirits with authority and power, and they come out." And his fame went out to every place in the surrounding countryside.

They came out of the synagogue and entered into the house of Simon and Andrew, with James and John. But Simon's

Speaking with Authority
in Capernaum

Mark 1:21-28
Luke 4:31-37

Carrying Our Sicknesses

Matt. 8:14-17
Mark 1:29-34
Luke 4:38-41

wife's mother lay sick of a fever. When they told Jesus about her, he stood over her, took her by the hand, rebuked the fever, and lifted her up. Immediately, the fever left her and she served them.

In the evening, as the sun was setting, they brought to him all the people who were diseased, and those possessed with devils. He laid his hands on every one of them, and healed them. All the town was gathered at the door and he healed many that were sick of a variety of diseases. Devils also came out of many people, crying out, "You are Christ, the Son of God." Jesus rebuked them and did not allow them to speak, because they knew that he was Christ. This fulfilled the words of Isaiah the prophet, who had said, "He took our infirmities, and bore our sicknesses."

Touring with the Gospel

Matt. 4:23-25
Mark 1:35-39
Luke 4:42-44;
5:12-16

In the morning, rising up well before daylight, he went out to a solitary place and prayed. Simon and those with him followed along. When they found him, they said, "Everyone is looking for you." People looked for him, came to him, and prevented him from leaving them. He told them, "I must preach the kingdom of God in other towns as well. This is why I was sent here." And he preached in synagogues throughout Galilee, and cast out devils. His fame extended throughout Syria and they brought to him people who were afflicted with diseases, possessed with devils, mentally disturbed, and paralyzed. He healed them all.

Huge crowds of people from Galilee, Decapolis, Jerusalem, Judea, and from beyond Jordan followed him. And it so happened that when Jesus was in a certain town, a man covered with leprosy saw him. He fell on his face and begged him, "Lord, if you want, you can make me clean." Jesus reached out his hand, touched him, and said, "I will. Be clean." Immediately the man's leprosy was gone. Jesus ordered him not to tell anyone. "Go to the priest," he said, "and make an offering for your cleansing, just as Moses commanded. This is proof of your cleansing."

As the man went on his way, he told everyone what had happened to him. Then such crowds surrounded Jesus that he couldn't even enter the towns publicly.

So he stayed in secluded places and prayed. Still, people from everywhere came to him.

The Hostility from Religious Leaders
in Capernaum

Forgiving Sin

Matt. 9:1-8
Mark 2:1-12
Luke 5:17-26

After a few days, he went back to Capernaum and people learned that he was at home. Immediately, many gathered together there, but there was no room for them, not even outside near the door. He preached the word to them and the power of the Lord was present to heal them.

It so happened that, as he was teaching, Pharisees and doctors of the law were listening. They had come out of every town in Galilee and Judea, including Jerusalem. And men brought a man in a bed, who was paralyzed. They looked for a way to bring him into the house to Jesus. When they could not find a way because of the crowds, they went up on the housetop, broke open the roof, and let the man down on his bed. And there he was in the middle of the room in front of Jesus. When Jesus saw their faith, he said to the paralyzed man, "Your sins are forgiven."

The scribes and the Pharisees reasoned in their hearts: "Who is this man who speaks blasphemies? Who can forgive sins? Only God." Jesus knew their thoughts and said to them, "What are you thinking? Which is easier to say, 'Your sins are forgiven;' or 'Rise up, take your bed, and walk?' But I want you to know that the Son of Man has power on earth to forgive sins." Then he said to the paralyzed man, "Get up, take your bed, and go to your house." Immediately, he stood up in front of them all, picked up his bed, and left for his house, glorifying God. Everyone was amazed and glorified God. "We have never seen anything like this," they said.

He went out again to the lakeshore. There the crowd came to him, and he taught them. As he walked along, he saw Levi, the son of Alphaeus, sitting at a customs table collecting taxes. Jesus said to him, "Follow me." And Levi stood up, left it all, and followed Jesus.

Then Levi had a big celebration for Jesus in his own house. Many tax collectors and others sat down with them to eat. When the scribes and Pharisees saw him eating with tax collectors and sinners, they

Feasting
with Sinners

Matt. 9:9-13
Mark 2:13-17
Luke 5:27-32

said to his disciples, "How can he eat and drink with publicans and sinners?"

When Jesus heard this, he said to them, "It is not those who are healthy who need a doctor, but those who are sick. So go and figure out what this means: 'I want mercy, not sacrifice.' I came to call sinners to repentance, not the righteous."

Working on the Sabbath
in Jerusalem

John 5:1-15

After this, Jesus went up to Jerusalem for a Jewish feast.

At Jerusalem, by the sheep market, there was a pool, called Bethesda, with five covered porches. In these porches lay a big crowd of sick people—blind, lame, or paralyzed—waiting for the water to move. (They believed that an angel went down into the pool and stirred up the water at a certain time. When this happened, whoever stepped into the water first was healed of his disease.)

A man was there who had been sick for thirty-eight years. Jesus saw him and knew that he had been sick a long time. Jesus said to him, "Do you want to be made whole?" The sick man answered, "Sir, when the water is stirred, I have no one to put me into the pool. While I am coming down to the water, someone else steps in before me." Jesus said to him, "Get up, take your bed, and walk." Immediately the man was cured, picked up his bed, and walked.

That day was the Sabbath. So the Jewish leaders said to the man who was cured, "It is the Sabbath. It is not legal for you to carry your bed." He answered them, "The man that healed me said to me, 'Take your bed and walk.' " Then they asked him, "Who told you, 'Take your bed and walk?'" The man did not know who it was. (Jesus had gone away because there was a crowd of people there.) Afterward, Jesus found the man in the temple, and said to him, "Look, you are cured. Sin no more, or else something worse might happen to you." The man left and told the Jewish leaders that it was Jesus who had healed him.

So the religious leaders persecuted Jesus and wanted to kill him, because he had done these things on the Sabbath. Jesus told them, "My Father works until now, and I work too." Therefore, they sought

Identifying Himself as God's Son

John 5:16-30

to kill him even more—not only had he broken the Sabbath, but he said that God was his Father, making himself equal with God.

Jesus said to them, "I'll tell you the truth, the Son can do nothing by himself. He does what he sees the Father doing. The things the Father does, the Son does likewise. Because the Father loves the Son, and shows him all the things that he does. You will marvel because he will show the Son greater works than these. Just as the Father raises the dead and gives them life, so the Son gives life to whomever he wants. The Father judges no one, but has given all judgment to the Son, so that everyone would honor the Son, just as they honor the Father. Whoever does not honor the Son does not honor the Father who has sent him.

"Here is the truth: Whoever hears my word and believes in him that sent me, has eternal life and will not be condemned, but is passed from death to life. I'll tell you the truth, the time is coming—in fact, it has arrived—when the dead will hear the voice of the Son of God. They who hear it will live. For just as the Father has life in himself; so he has given that life to the Son and has given him authority to execute judgment. Why? Because he is the Son of Man. Do not marvel at this, because the time is coming when all those in the grave will hear his voice, and will come out—they who have done good, to the resurrection of life; and they who have done evil, to the resurrection of damnation. I can do nothing alone—I hear and I judge, and my judgment is just, because I do not seek my own will, but the will of the Father, who has sent me.

If I alone tell you about myself, the things I say are not true. But there is another person who testifies for me, and I know that his testimony is true. You asked John, and he told you the truth. I do not need the testimony of a man. But I am telling you these things so that you can be saved. He was a burning and a shining light and you were willing, for a time, to rejoice in his light. But something greater than John speaks for me: It is the work which the Father has given me to finish. I do this

The Witnesses to His Sonship

John 5:31-47

work and it tells you that the Father has sent me.

"And the Father himself, who sent me, has told you about me. You have never heard his voice or seen his shape. And you do not have his word living in you, because you do not believe me, the man he sent. You study the Scriptures because you think you can find eternal life in them. They tell you about me, yet you will not come to me so that you can have eternal life.

"I do not receive honor from people, but I know you and that you do not have the love of God in you. I have come in my Father's name, and you do not receive me. But if someone else comes in his own name, you will receive him. No wonder you can't believe. You receive honor from each other, yet you do not desire the honor that can come only from God.

"Don't think that I will accuse you to the Father. There is only one who will accuse you—Moses, the one you trust. If you had believed Moses, you would have believed me, because he wrote about me. But if you do not believe his writings, how will you believe my words?"

At that time, Jesus went out through the wheat fields on the Sabbath day. His disciples were hungry and picked the wheat to eat. When the Pharisees saw this they said to him, "Look, your disciples are doing something that is not legal to do on the Sabbath." But he said to them, "Haven't you read what David did, when he and those with him were hungry? He entered into the house of God and ate the ceremonial bread, which was not lawful for him to eat. Only the priests could eat it. Or haven't you read in the law, how on the Sabbath days the priests in the temple profane the Sabbath and are blameless?

"I tell you, here in this place is a man who is greater than the temple. But if you had known what this means: 'I will have mercy, and not sacrifice,' you would not have condemned the innocent. For the Son of Man is the Lord of the Sabbath."

On another Sabbath, Jesus went into the synagogue and taught. There was a man whose right hand was withered. They asked Jesus, "Is it lawful to heal on the Sabbath?" (They asked this because they

Ruling the Sabbath

Matt. 12:1-8
Mark 2:23-28
Luke 6:1-5

Working on the Sabbath Again

Matt. 12:9-14
Mark 3:1-6
Luke 6:6-11

wanted to accuse him of breaking the religious law.) He said to them, "If your sheep falls into a pit on the Sabbath, wouldn't you lift it out?

"How much better is a man than a sheep? So you see, it is lawful to do good on the Sabbath." Still, the scribes and Pharisees watched to see if he would heal on the Sabbath, because they wanted to accuse him. He knew their thoughts, however, and said to the man who had the withered hand, "Get up, and stand where everyone can see you." The man stepped forward.

Then Jesus said to them, "I will ask you one thing; is it lawful to do good on the Sabbath, or to do evil? To save life, or to destroy it?" But they said nothing. And looking around at them all, he said to the man, "Stretch out your hand." He did so, and his hand was restored whole, like the other. The Pharisees were filled with anger and consulted each other about how they could destroy Jesus.

CHAPTER FOUR

HIS WORK
IN GALILEE CONTINUES

**The Crowds
Follow Him**

*Matt. 12:15-
21
Mark 3:7-12*

When Jesus learned that they wanted to kill him, he withdrew from Jerusalem. Huge crowds from Galilee, Judea, Jerusalem, Idumea, beyond Jordan, and Tyre and Sidon followed him when they heard of the wonderful things he did. Jesus asked his disciples that a small boat should wait for him in case the crowd rushed at him. (He had healed so many people that those who had diseases pushed and shoved just to touch him.) When unclean spirits saw him, they fell down in front of him, and cried, "You are the Son of God."

And he commanded that they not reveal this fact.

This fulfilled the words spoken by Isaiah the prophet: "Look at my servant, whom I have chosen—my beloved, in whom my soul is well pleased. I will put my spirit upon him, and he will show judgment to the Gentiles. He will not strive or cry out; nor will anyone hear his voice calling in the streets. He will not break a bruised reed nor will he extinguish smoking flax, until justice arrives with his final victory. And the whole world will trust in his name."

Designating the Apostles
in Capernaum

Matt. 10:2-4
Mark 3:13-19
Luke 6:12-19

Jesus went out to a mountain to pray, and continued all night in prayer to God. When it was day, he called his disciples. From among them he chose twelve to be with him, so that he could send them out to preach, and to have power to heal sicknesses, and to cast out devils.

These are the apostles he chose: Simon (whom he also named Peter), and Andrew his brother, James and John (he named them Boanerges, which means "sons of thunder"), Philip and Bartholomew,

Matthew and Thomas, James the son of Alphaeus, and Simon the Canaanite, Judas the brother of James, and Judas Iscariot (who was the traitor).

He came down the mountain with them and stood in the plain with the rest of his disciples where a big crowd of people had come, from Judea and Jerusalem, and from the lake coast of Tyre and Sidon, to hear him and to be healed of their diseases. People who were troubled with unclean spirits were healed. The whole crowd wanted to touch him, because purity went out of him when they did this. He healed them all.

Seeing the crowds, Jesus went up on a hill. When he sat down, his disciples came to him and he taught them:

"Blessed are the poor in spirit, for theirs is the kingdom of heaven. Blessed are those who mourn, for they will be comforted. Blessed are the meek, for they will inherit the earth. Blessed are those who hunger and thirst for righteousness, for they will be filled. Blessed are the merciful, for they will obtain mercy. Blessed

Teaching the Apostles

Matt. 5:1-7:28
Luke 6:20-49

are the pure in heart, for they will see God. Blessed are the peacemakers, for they will be called the children of God. Blessed are those who are persecuted for righteousness's sake, for theirs is the kingdom of heaven. Blessed are you when people revile and persecute you and say all kinds of evil things against you falsely because of me. Rejoice, be glad, because your reward in heaven is great. In the same way, they persecuted the prophets who came before you.

The Believers' Nature

You are the salt of the earth; but if the salt has lost its savor, it is good for nothing but to be cast out and be walked on like dust. You are the light of the world. A city set on a hill cannot be hidden. Neither do men light a candle, and put it under a basket. Instead, they put it on a candlestick, and it gives light to everyone in the house. Let your light shine before other people, so that they may see your good works and glorify your Father in heaven.

Fulfilling the Law

Do not think that I have come to destroy the law or the prophets. I have not come to destroy, but to fulfill them. Here is the truth, until heaven and earth end, not one jot or one mark will be deleted from the law, until it is all fulfilled. Whoever breaks one of the smallest commandments, and likewise teaches others to do so, will be the least in the kingdom of heaven; but whoever keeps and teaches these commandments will be great in the kingdom of heaven. I tell you, unless your righteousness is greater than the righteousness of the scribes and Pharisees, you will not enter the kingdom of heaven.

You have heard it said, 'You shall not kill'; and 'whoever kills will be in danger of the judgment.' But I say to you that whoever is angry without a cause will be in danger of the judgment. Whoever will say to his brother, 'Idiot!' is in danger of the council's judgment. But whoever will say 'You fool!' will be in danger of hell's fire.

Anger

"Therefore if you bring your gift to the altar, and there remember that your brother has something against you, leave your gift there at the altar and go be reconciled to your brother, then come and offer your gift. Agree with your opponent quickly, while you are with him, just in case he brings you to a judge, and the judge gives you over to an officer, and you are cast into prison. I tell you the truth, you shall not come out until you have paid the last penny.

Adultery

You have heard it said, 'You shall not commit adultery.' But I say to you that whoever looks with lust at a woman has committed adultery with her in his heart.

"If your right eye offends you, pluck it out and cast it away. It is better that one of your members would perish than for your whole body to be cast into hell. If your right hand offends you, cut it off and cast it away. It is better that one of your members perish rather than your whole body be cast into hell.

"It has been said, 'Whoever wants to divorce his wife must give her a letter of divorce.' But I say that whoever divorces his wife, except for fornication, causes her to commit adultery; and whoever marries her commits adultery.

You have heard it said, 'You shall not swear, but shall perform your oaths to the Lord.' But I say, Don't swear at all: not by heaven—it is God's throne; nor by the earth—it is his footstool; neither by Jerusalem—it is the city of the great King. Do not swear by your head either, because you cannot make one hair white or black. Instead, say either 'Yes, I will,' or 'No, I won't.' To strengthen this by swearing with an oath is wrong.

Oaths

You have heard it said, 'An eye for an eye, and a tooth for a tooth.' But I say, do not resist evil. Whoever hits you on your right cheek, turn the other cheek to him also. And if anyone sues you and takes away your coat, let him have your cloak also. And whoever compels you to go a mile, go with him two. Give to him who asks, and do not turn away from a borrower.

Revenge

You have heard it said, 'You will love your neighbor, and hate your enemy.' But I say to you, Love your enemies, bless those who curse you, do good to those who hate you, and pray for those who are

Love

dishonest with you, and persecute you. In this way you are the children of your Father in heaven—who makes the sun rise on the evil and on the good, and sends rain on the just and on the unjust. For if you only love those who love you, what reward do you have? Don't the tax collectors do this? And if you only greet your friends, you are like everyone else. But you are to be as perfect as your Father in heaven is perfect.

The Way
to Give

Take care that you do not give money so that others will see you do it. Otherwise you will have no reward from your Father who is in heaven. When you give money, do not make a show of it like the hypocrites do in the synagogues and in the streets, so that they can have human glory. Here is the truth: They have their reward. But when you give, do not let your left hand know what your right hand is doing. Then your giving will be in secret and your Father who sees in secret will reward you openly.

When you pray, do not be like the hypocrites. They love to pray publicly, standing in the synagogues and on the corners of the streets so that they will be seen. I'll tell you the truth, they have their reward. But when you pray, go into a private room, and when you have shut the door, pray to your Father who is in secret. And your Father, who sees in secret, will reward you openly.

"When you pray, do not vainly repeat yourself, like people in other religions do. They think that they will be heard if they say a lot. Do not be like them. Your Father knows what you need before you ask.

"Pray like this: Our Father who is in heaven, may your name be holy. May your kingdom come, and your will be done on earth, as it is in heaven. Give us today our daily bread. And forgive us our sins, as we forgive those who have sinned against us. And do not allow us to be tempted, but deliver us from evil: For the kingdom, and the power, and the glory are yours forever. Amen.

"For if you forgive others their sins, your heavenly Father will also forgive you. But if you do not forgive others their sins, neither will your Father forgive your transgressions.

"Moreover, when you fast, do not be sad like the hypocrites. They frown so that they appear to others to be fasting. I say to you, they have their reward. But when you fast, anoint your head, and wash your face so that you do not appear to be fasting except to your Father who is in secret. And your Father, who sees in secret, will reward you openly.

Wealth and Possessions

Do not hoard treasures for yourself on earth, where moths and rust can ruin them and where thieves can break in and steal them. But deposit treasures in heaven, where moths and rust can not ruin them and where thieves can not break in and steal them. For where your treasure is, there will your heart be also.

"The light of the body is the eye. Therefore if your eye is single, your whole body will be full of light. But if your eye is evil, your whole body will be full of darkness. If the light that is in you is darkness, how great is that darkness!

"No one can serve two masters. Either

he will hate one, and love the other; or else he will hold on to one and despise the other. You cannot serve God and mammon. This is why I say, do not worry about your life, what you will eat, or what you will drink; or what you will wear. Isn't life more than food, and your body more than clothing?

"Look at the birds flying in the air. They do not sow seed, or harvest and gather crops into barns, yet your heavenly Father feeds them. Aren't you much better than they? Which of you by worrying can add one inch to his height? And why do you worry about clothes? Think about the lilies of the field. They do not work or spin cloth. Yet even Solomon in all his glory was not clothed like them.

"Therefore, if God clothes the grass of the field, which today is here and tomorrow is burned, won't he clothe you? O you of little faith? Therefore, do not worry, saying, 'What will we eat?' or 'What will we drink?' or 'What will we wear?' (After all, unbelievers seek after all these things.) Your heavenly Father knows that you need all these things. But first, seek the kingdom of God and the right-eousness of God. Then all these things will be given to you. Do not worry about tomorrow, for tomorrow will worry about itself. One day's worth of evil is enough.

Condemning Others

Don't judge others; then you will not be judged. For you will be judged by the standard you use for others. The measure you use will be applied to you. Why do you worry about the speck in your brother's eye, but not the log that is in your own eye? Or can you say to your brother, 'Let me pull the speck out of your eye?' Look! A log is in your own eye. You hypocrite, first cast the log out of your own eye. Then you will be able to see clearly to cast the speck out of your brother's eye. Do not give holy things to unholy people; do not give pearls to swine, they will trample them under their feet, turn, and attack you.

Persevering in Prayer

Ask, and it will be given to you; seek, and you will find; knock, and the door will be opened to you: Because everyone that asks, receives; and the person that seeks, finds; and when you knock, it will be opened. If your son asks for bread, do you give him a stone? Or if he asks for a fish, will you give him a serpent? If you who are evil know how to give good gifts to your children, how much more will your Father who is in heaven give good things to those who ask? Therefore, everything you want people to do to you, do so to them. This will fulfill all the law and words of the prophets.

Enter in at the narrow gate. The gate is wide and the way is broad that leads to destruction, and many go in that way. But the gate is small and the way is narrow that leads to life, and few find it.

False Prophets

"Beware of false prophets who come to you in sheep's clothing. Inwardly they are hungry wolves. You will recognize them by their fruits. Do people gather grapes from thorny vines, or figs from thistles? No. Every good tree produces good fruit. A corrupt tree produces bad fruit. A good tree cannot produce bad fruit, neither can a corrupt tree produce good fruit. Every tree that does not produce good fruit is cut down and cast into the fire. Therefore, you will know them by their fruits.

Not every one who calls me Lord will enter into the kingdom of heaven; only the ones who do the will of my Father who is in heaven. Many will say to me in that day, 'Lord, Lord, have we not prophesied in your name? And in your name cast out devils? And in your name done many wonderful works?' Then will I tell them, 'I never knew you. Get away from me, you evil workers.'

"Therefore, whoever hears my sayings, and does them, is like a wise man who built his house upon a rock. The rain came down, and the floods came up, and the winds blew and beat upon that house; and it did not fall, because it was founded upon a rock. Everyone who hears these sayings and does not do them is like a foolish man who built his house upon the sand. The rain came down, the floods came up, and the winds blew and beat upon that house, and it fell with a great crash."

When Jesus finished talking, the people

were astonished, because he taught them with authority, not like the scribes.

H e finished teaching them and went back to Capernaum. A Roman military officer who lived there had a servant who was dear to him, but was sick, and ready to die. And when the officer heard of Jesus, he sent the Jewish elders to ask him to come and heal his servant. When they came to Jesus, they begged him to come, claiming that the centurion was worthy: "For he loves our nation, and he has built us a synagogue."

Jesus went with them. When he was not far from the house, the centurion sent friends to him, saying, "Lord, do not trouble yourself. I am not worthy for you to enter under my roof. This is why I did not come to you myself. Just speak a word and my servant will be healed. For I am also a man under authority, and I have under me soldiers. I say to one, 'Go,' and he goes; and to another, 'Come,' and he comes; and to my servant, 'Do this,' and he does it."

When Jesus heard this, he marveled at

Finding a Gentile's Remarkable Faith
in Capernaum

Matt. 8:5-13
Luke 7:1-10

the officer and said to the people who were following him, "I have not found someone with such remarkable faith in all of Israel. I tell you, many will come from the east and west, and will sit down with Abraham, and Isaac, and Jacob, in the kingdom of heaven. But the children of the kingdom will be cast into outer darkness where there will be weeping and gnashing of teeth."

And they returned to the officer's house and found that the servant who had been sick was well.

Sympathizing with Suffering
in Nain

Luke 7:11-17

It so happened that, the next day, he went into a town called Nain. Many of his disciples and many people went with him. When he came near the town gate, there was a dead man being carried out. This man was the only son of his widowed mother. Many people of the town were with her. The Lord saw her, had compassion on her, and said, "Don't cry." He touched the coffin and those carrying it stopped. He said, "Young man, I say, get up." And the dead man sat up and began to speak. Jesus led him to his mother.

All who saw this were afraid and they glorified God: "A great prophet is risen up among us," they declared. "God has visited his people." This story spread throughout the region of Judea.

In prison, John heard about the things Christ was doing. So he sent two of his disciples to ask him, "Are you the coming one? Or should we look for someone else?" At that very time, Jesus cured many people's sicknesses, diseases, and evil spirits. He gave sight to many people who were blind.

Playing the Flute and Singing a Dirge
in Bethsaida

Matt. 11:2-24
Luke 7:18-35

Jesus answered John's disciples, "Go on your way and tell John the things you have seen and heard here; how the blind see, the lame walk, the lepers are cleansed, the deaf hear, the dead are raised, and the gospel is preached to the poor. Tell him, 'Blessed is he who does not stumble on account of me.'"

When the men departed, Jesus spoke to the people about John: "What did you go out into the wilderness to see; a reed shaken with the wind? What did you go out to see; a man dressed in soft clothes?

Look, those who wear gorgeous clothes and live delicately are in kings' courts. So what did you go out there to see; a prophet? Yes, and I tell you, he is much more than a prophet. This is the man about whom is written, 'Look, I send my messenger before you, who will prepare the way for you.'

"I tell you, of all people ever born, there is not a greater prophet than John the Baptist. But whoever is the least member of the kingdom of God is greater than John.

"From the days of John the Baptist until now, eager people have been rushing into the kingdom; because the prophets and the law spoke about the time when John came. And if you can, understand this: He is Elijah—the one the prophets said would come."

All the people and the tax collectors that heard him agreed because they were baptized by John. But the Pharisees and lawyers rejected this information from God because they were not baptized by John.

And the Lord said, "What are the people of this generation like? They are like children sitting in the marketplace, calling one to another, saying:

> We have played the flute,
>> and you have not danced;
> We have sung a dirge,
>> and you have not wept.

"Because John the Baptist did not eat bread or drink wine, you said, 'He has a devil.' But the Son of Man has come eating and drinking, and you say, 'Look! a glutton and a drunk, a friend of publicans and sinners!' But wisdom is known by its results."

Then he began to rebuke the towns where most of his mighty works had been done, because they did not repent: "Woe to you, Chorazin! Woe to you, Bethsaida! For if the mighty works that were done in you had been done in Tyre and Sidon, they would have repented long ago in sackcloth and ashes. But I say to you, it will be more tolerable for Tyre and Sidon at the day of judgment than for you.

"And you, Capernaum, which is exalted to heaven, you will be brought down to hell. For if the mighty works that have been done in you had been done in Sodom, it would have remained until this day. But I say to you that it will be more tolerable for the land of Sodom in the day of judgment than for you."

Offering Rest to the Weary

Matt. 11:25-30

Then Jesus prayed, "I thank you, O Father, Lord of heaven and earth, because you have hidden these things from the wise and prudent, and have revealed them to babes. This seemed good in your sight.

"All things are given to me by my Father; no one knows the Son, but the Father; neither does anyone know the Father except the Son and whoever is shown the Father by the Son.

"Come to me, all you who labor and are heavy laden, and I will give you rest. Take my yoke upon you, and learn from me, because I am meek and lowly in heart; and you will find rest for your souls. My yoke is easy, and my burden is light."

Many Sins, Much Love

Luke 7:36-50

One of the Pharisees wanted Jesus to eat with him. So Jesus went into the Pharisee's house, and sat down to eat. A woman in the town, who was a sinner, knew that

Jesus was eating in the Pharisee's house. So she brought an alabaster jar of ointment and stood at Jesus' feet behind him, weeping, and washed his feet with her tears, wiped them with her hair, kissed his feet, and anointed them with the ointment.

When the Pharisee saw this, he thought, "If this man were a prophet, he would have known who this woman is and what kind of person it is that is touching him—she is a sinner." And Jesus said to him, "Simon, I have something to say to you." And he said, "Master, I am listening."

"There was a certain creditor who had two debtors: One owed five hundred dollars, and the other fifty. When they had nothing to pay, he canceled the debt for both of them. Tell me, which of the debtors will love him most?" Simon answered, "I suppose the one whom he forgave most." And Jesus said to him, "You are right."

Jesus turned to the woman and said to Simon, "Do you see this woman? When I entered your house, you gave me no water for my feet. But she has washed my feet with her tears and wiped them with her hair. You gave me no kiss. But this woman, since the time I came in, has not ceased kissing my feet. You did not anoint my head with oil. But this woman has anointed my feet with ointment. Her many sins are forgiven, because she loved much. But to whom little is forgiven, the same person loves little."

And he said to the woman, "Your sins are forgiven." The others at the table eating with him thought to themselves, "Who is this that forgives sins?"

And he said to the woman, "Your faith has saved you; go in peace."

The Women of the Work

Luke 8:1-3

After this, he went throughout every town and village, preaching the good news of the kingdom of God. The twelve disciples were with him, and some women who had been healed of evil spirits and sicknesses. These included Mary called Magdalene, out of whom he cast seven devils, Joanna the wife of Chuza (Herod's steward), Susanna, and many others who ministered to him from their own resources.

The crowd pressed them so that they could not so much as eat a meal. And when his relatives heard of it they went out to lay hold of him. They said, "He has lost his senses."

The Blasphemy of the Religious Leaders
near the Sea of Galilee

Matt. 12:22-37
Mark 3:20-30

Then someone brought to him a man possessed with a devil—blind and dumb. He healed him so that he could both speak and see. And all the people were amazed and said, "Is not this the son of David?" But the scribes who came down from Jerusalem said, "He is Satanic, and by the prince of the devils he casts out devils."

Jesus knew their thoughts and said to them, "Every kingdom divided against itself is brought to desolation; and every city or house divided against itself will not stand. If Satan casts out Satan, he is divided against himself; how will his kingdom stand? And if I by Beelzebub cast out devils, by whom do your followers cast them out? Therefore, they will be your judges. But if I cast out devils by the Spirit of God, then the kingdom of God is come to you. How can one enter into a strong man's house and spoil his goods except he first tie up the strong man? Only then can he rob his house.

"He that is not with me is against me; and he that does not gather with me, scatters. Therefore, I say, all manner of sin and blasphemy will be forgiven to men, but the blasphemy against the Holy Spirit will not be forgiven. It will be forgiven if someone speaks a word against the Son of Man. But whoever speaks against the Holy Spirit, this will not be forgiven, not in this world and not in the world to come." (Because they said, 'He has an unclean spirit.') "Either make the tree good, and its fruit good; or else make the tree corrupt, and its fruit corrupt: for the tree is known by its fruit.

"O generation of snakes, how can you, being evil, speak good things? For out of the abundance of the heart the mouth speaks. A good man out of the good treasure of the heart produces good things: and an evil man out of the evil treasure produces evil things. But I say to you that, in the day of judgment, people will give account for every idle word they speak. For by your words you will be justified, and by your words you will be condemned."

Then some of the scribes and the Pharisees answered, "Master, we want to see you perform a miraculous sign." But he said to them, "An evil and adulterous generation seeks a sign. There will not be a sign given to it, except the sign of the prophet Jonah.

"Jonah was three days and three nights in the whale's belly; so will the Son of Man be three days and three nights in the heart of the earth. The men of Nineveh will rise with this generation at the time of judgment and will condemn you, because they repented at the preaching of Jonah. Look! A greater prophet than Jonah is here.

"The queen of the south will rise up in the time of judgment with this generation, and will condemn you; for she came from the most distant region of the world to hear the wisdom of Solomon; and look! a greater man than Solomon is here.

"When an unclean spirit is gone out of a person, the spirit walks through dry places seeking rest and finds none. Then he says, 'I will return to my house where I came from.' When he comes back to the person's soul, he finds it empty, swept, and pleasant. Then he takes seven other spirits more wicked than himself, and together they enter and dwell there. The last state of that person is worse than the first. So it will be with this wicked generation."

The Family of God

Matt. 12:46-50
Mark 3:31-35
Luke 8:19-21

While he talked to the people, his mother and his brothers stood outside desiring to speak with him. But the crowd sat close around him. They said to him, "Look, your mother and your brothers are outside, wanting to speak with you."

He answered, "Who is my mother? Who are my brothers?" He stretched out his hand toward his disciples and said, "Look at my mother and my brothers! Whoever does my Father's will, they are my brother, and sister, and mother."

Teaching the People *in Capernaum*

The Parable of Four Soils

Matt. 13:1-9
Mark 4:1-20
Luke 8:4-8

That day, Jesus went out and sat by the lakeside. And great crowds gathered around him. So he boarded a boat and sat there and the crowd stood on the shore.

He spoke many things to them in parables:

"A farmer went out to sow seed; and when he sowed, some seeds fell by the wayside, and the birds came and devoured them. Some fell on stony places where there was not much earth. Soon they sprang up because they had no depth of soil. When the sun was up, they were scorched. Because they had no root, they withered away.

"Some seeds fell among thorns. The thorns grew up and choked them. But other seeds fell into good ground and produced fruit. Some produced thirty, others sixty, and some even a hundred times as much as had been planted. Whoever wants to understand this must listen carefully."

The disciples came and said, "Why do you speak to them in parables?" He said, "Because you have been permitted to understand the mysteries of the kingdom of heaven, but they cannot understand. Whoever has this understanding will be given more, and will have an abundance of knowledge. But whoever is not listening will lose even what understanding he has. Here is why I speak in parables: While seeing me, they do not actually see. They hear what I say, but are not really listening, nor do they understand. They fulfilled the prophecy of Isaiah, who said, 'By hearing you will hear, and will not understand; and seeing you will see, and will not perceive. For this people's heart is hard and their ears are dull of hearing and their eyes have closed, lest at any time they should see with their eyes and hear with their ears, and should understand with their heart, be converted, and I could heal them.'

"But your eyes are blessed, because they see, and your ears also, for they hear. For I tell you the truth, many prophets and righteous men have desired to see the things that you see, and have not seen them; and to hear the things that you hear, and have not heard them.

"Listen to the meaning of the parable of the farmer:

"When any one hears the word of the kingdom and does not understand it, then the wicked one comes, and takes away that which was sown in his heart. This is like the seed by the wayside. The seed in stony places is sown in a person who hears the word and with joy receives it, yet he has no depth of soul. So when tribulation or persecution comes up because of the word, he falls away.

"The seed sown among the thorns is like a person who hears the word, but the cares of this world and the deceitfulness of riches choke it and he becomes unfruitful. But the seed in the good ground is like a person who hears the word and understands it; who also bears fruit, producing thirty, sixty, even a hundred times as much as had been planted.

The kingdom of God is like a man who plants seed in the ground, goes to sleep, rises night and day, and goes about his business. The seed springs up and grows, but he does not know how it does this, because the earth produces fruit all by itself; first the blade, then the ear, after that the full corn in the ear. When the fruit is produced, immediately the man begins to cut the crop, because the harvest has come."

The Parable of Growth and Harvest

Mark 4:26-29

He told them another parable: "The kingdom of heaven is like a man who sowed good seed in his field. But while he slept, his enemy came and sowed tares

The Parable of Wheat and Tares

Matt. 13:24-30

among the wheat, and went his way.

"When the blade was sprung up and brought forth fruit, the tares appeared as well. So the man's servants said to him, 'Sir, didn't you sow good seed in your field? Why are tares growing in it?' He said to them, 'An enemy has done this.' The servants said, 'Do you want us to gather up the tares?'

"He said, 'No. Because while you gather up the tares, you will root up the wheat with them. Let both grow together until the harvest. In the time of harvest, I will say to the reapers, 'First gather together the tares and bind them in bundles to burn them; but gather the wheat into my barn.' "

The Parable of Mustard Seed

Matt. 13:31-32
Mark 4:30-34

Jesus told them another parable: "The kingdom of heaven is like a grain of mustard seed, which a man sowed in his field. It is among the smallest of all seeds, but when it is grown, it is the greatest among herbs and becomes a tree, so that the birds of the air come and live in its branches." Using many parables like this, he spoke the word as the people were able to hear it. But he did not speak to them without using parables. And he explained everything to his disciples when they were alone.

He told them another parable: "The kingdom of heaven is like leaven that a woman mixed into three measures of meal. Eventually, all the meal was leavened." Jesus spoke all these things to the crowd using parables. And he did not speak to them without using parables, thus fulfilling the words of the prophet who said, "I will open my mouth in parables; I will speak things which have been kept secret from the beginning of the world."

The Parable of Yeast

Matt. 13:33-35

Jesus sent the crowd away and went into the house. His disciples came to him, saying, "Explain to us the parable of the tares in the field."

He said, "The one who plants the good seed is the Son of Man; the field is the world; the good seed are the children of the kingdom, but the tares are the children of the wicked one. The enemy that sowed them is the devil; the harvest is the end of

Explaining the Parable of Wheat and Tares

Matt. 13:36-43

the world; and the reapers are the angels.

"The tares are gathered and burned, and so will it be at the end of the world. The Son of Man will send his angels, they will gather from his kingdom all the things in it that are an offense, and all those who do evil, and will throw them into the fire. There will be wailing and gnashing of teeth. Then the righteous people will shine like the sun in the kingdom of their Father. Whoever is willing should listen and understand.

The Parables of Treasure, Pearls, and Harvest

Matt. 13:44-52

The kingdom of heaven is like treasure hidden in a field. When a man finds it, he hides it again and with joy goes and sells all that he has and buys the field.

"The kingdom of heaven is like a merchant seeking valuable pearls, who, when he finds one rare pearl, sells all that he has, and buys it.

"The kingdom of heaven is like a net in the lake filled with all kinds of fish. When it is full, fishermen pull it to shore, sit down, gather in the good fish, but throw the bad ones away. It will be like this at the end of the world. The angels will come, cut the wicked people off from the righteous ones, and cast them into the fire. There will be wailing and gnashing of teeth."

Jesus said to them, "Have you understood all these things?" They said to him, "Yes, Lord." So he said, "Every student who is taught about the kingdom of heaven is like a person who brings out of storage things that are both new and old."

The same day, when evening came, he said to them, "Let us cross over to the other side of the lake." They sent away the crowd and took him aboard a boat. Other boats followed.

A big storm blew in, and waves broke over the boat and filled it with water. Jesus was in the rear part of the boat, asleep on a cushion. They awakened him, and said, "Master, don't you care that we are going to drown?"

Jesus got up, rebuked the wind, and said to the lake, "Peace. Be still." The wind stopped and there was a great calm. Then he said to them, "Why are you so afraid? Why don't you have any faith?"

Touring with the Gospel Again

Ruling the Wind and the Water *on the Sea of Galilee*

Matt. 8:23-27
Mark 4:35-41
Luke 8:22-25

They became even more afraid and said to each other, "What kind of man is this? Even the wind and the water obey him!"

They came to the other side of the lake, to the country of the Gadarenes, which borders Galilee. When he came out of the boat, he met a man with an unclean spirit, who had lived among the tombs. No one could bind him, not even with chains. He had often been bound with ropes and chains, but he pulled the chains apart and broke the ropes in pieces. Nor could any one tame him. Night and day he was in the mountains and the tombs crying, and cutting himself with stones.

But when he saw Jesus from afar, he ran, worshipped him, and cried with a loud voice, "What have I to do with you, Jesus, Son of the most high God? I beg you by God, do not torment me," because Jesus had said to him, "Come out of the man, you unclean spirit." Jesus asked him, "What is your name?" He answered, "My name is Legion, because we are many." The demons begged that Jesus would not send them out of the country.

Nearby was a large herd of swine feeding in the mountains. All the demons begged Jesus, "Send us into the swine." And so Jesus did. The unclean spirits went out of the man, entered into the swine, and the herd ran violently down a steep place into the lake and were drowned, about two thousand of them.

The swineherders ran away and told about these events in the town and in the country. When the people went out to see what had happened, they came to Jesus, and saw the man who had been possessed with the legion of devils, sitting, clothed, and in his right mind. They were afraid. Those who had witnessed what happened told them about the man who was possessed with the devil, and also about the swine. So the people begged him to leave their country.

When Jesus boarded the boat, the man who had been possessed with the demons asked if he could go with him. Jesus would not allow this, but said, "Go home to your friends, and tell them about the great things the Lord has done for you, and how he has had compassion on you."

So the man went away and declared in Decapolis the great things Jesus had done for him; and everyone marveled.

Restoring Life
in Capernaum

Matt. 9:18-26
Mark 5:21-43
Luke 8:40-56

When Jesus had crossed to the other side of the lake in the boat, many people gathered around him. One of the leaders of the synagogue, named Jairus, came to him, fell at his feet, and desperately begged him, "My little daughter is at the point of death. I pray, come and lay your hands on her so that she can be healed and live."

Jesus went with him and many people followed and thronged him. A woman was there who had been bleeding for twelve years. She had suffered many things of many physicians, had spent all her money, yet was not helped at all, but rather had become worse. When she heard of Jesus, she came behind him in the press of the crowd and touched his garment. (She thought, "If I only touch his clothes, I will be healed.")

Immediately, the flow of her blood dried up, and she felt in her body that she was healed of the affliction. Jesus immediately knew that power had gone out of him. He turned around in the press of the crowd and said, "Who touched my clothes?" His disciples said, "You can see the crowd thronging around you. How can you say, 'Who touched me?'"

He looked around to see who had done this. The woman, fearing, trembling, knowing what had been done in her, came and fell down in front of him and told him the truth. He said to her, "Daughter, your faith has healed you; go in peace, and be restored from your affliction."

While he was speaking, servants of the leader of the synagogue came to Jairus and said, "Your daughter is dead. Why do you trouble the Master?" Jesus heard what they said and told Jairus, "Do not be afraid, only believe." He allowed no one to follow him to Jairus's house except Peter, James, and John the brother of James.

When he came to the house and saw the confusion there and the people who wildly wept and wailed, he went in and said to them, "Why do you weep and make all this noise? The girl is not dead. She is asleep." They laughed at him scornfully. But he sent them all out of the house, took the father and the mother of the girl, and the disciples that were with him, and entered the room where the girl was lying.

He took her by the hand, and said to her, "Talitha kumi," which means, "Girl, I say to you, get up." Right away, the girl got up and walked. (She was twelve years old.) And they were absolutely astonished. Jesus told them to give the girl something to eat and commanded that no one should know what had happened. But his fame was broadcast into all the land.

When Jesus left the house, two blind men followed him, shouting, "Son of David, have mercy on us!" When he arrived at his house, the blind men came to him. Jesus said to them, "Do you believe that I am able to do this?" They said to him, "Yes, Lord." Then he touched their eyes, saying, "Let be it to you according to your faith." Their eyes were opened and they could see. Jesus strongly charged them, "See that no one knows about this." But when they went away, they spread his fame all around the countryside.

Just as they went out, some people brought to Jesus a man who could not speak and was possessed with a devil. The devil was cast out, the dumb man spoke, and the crowd marveled and declared, "This has never been seen before in Israel." But the Pharisees glowered, "He casts out devils by the power of the prince of the devils."

When Jesus finished teaching his parables, he left there and went to his hometown, where he taught in the synagogue. The people there were shocked and said, "Where did he get this wisdom and these mighty works?

"Isn't this the carpenter's son? Isn't his mother named Mary? And aren't his brothers James, Joseph, Simon, and Judas? And his sisters—aren't they all still living here? Where did Jesus get all this power and wisdom?" And they were offended. But Jesus said to them, "A prophet has honor everywhere except in his own country, and in his own house."

And he could do no miracles there

Rejected in His Hometown
in Nazareth

Matt. 13:53
Mark 6:1-6

(except he laid his hands upon a few of the sick and healed them). He was amazed at their unbelief.

Jesus went around all the towns and villages, teaching in the synagogues, preaching the gospel of the kingdom, and healing every sickness and every disease among the people. But when he saw the crowds, he was moved with love for them because they were weak and scattered—like sheep with no shepherd. Then he said to his disciples, "The harvest is abundant, but the laborers are few. Therefore, pray to the Lord of the harvest, that he will send laborers out to do the work of the harvest."

He called his twelve disciples and gave them power over unclean spirits—to cast them out—and to heal all kinds of sickness and all sorts of diseases.

Here are the names of the twelve apostles: First, Simon, who is called Peter, and Andrew his brother; James the son of Zebedee, and John his brother; Philip and Bartholomew; Thomas and Matthew the publican; James the son of Alphaeus, and Thaddaeus; Simon the Canaanite, and

Judas Iscariot, who betrayed him.

Jesus sent out these twelve and commanded them, "Do not go into the areas of the Gentiles or into any Samaritan town. Rather, go to the lost sheep of the house of Israel. And as you go, tell them this: 'The kingdom of heaven is at hand.' Heal the sick, cleanse the lepers, raise the dead, cast out devils. You have received all this for free, so freely give it to others. Do not carry gold, or silver, or brass in your pockets; take no money for your journey. Do not bring two coats, shoes, or a walking stick. A workman deserves to be fed.

"When you enter a town, ask who in it is worthy; stay with them until you leave. When you enter a house, greet those living there with God's peace. And if the house is worthy, let your peace remain there. But if it is not, take back your greeting. If a place does not receive you or hear your words, when you leave that house or town, shake the dust off of your feet. Here is the truth: In the day of judgment, it will be more tolerable for Sodom and Gomorrah than for that place.

I send you out like sheep among wolves. So be wise as serpents, and harmless as doves. But beware—men will bring you to trial, and they will whip you in the synagogues. You will be brought to judgment in front of governors and kings for my sake. There you will speak to them and to the whole world for me. But do not worry about how you will speak or what you will say. The words will be given to you at the time. Remember, it is not you that is speaking, it is the Spirit of your Father who speaks in you.

"A brother will betray his brother to death. The father will betray his child. The children will rebel against their parents and cause them to be put to death. And you will be hated by everyone because you follow me. But the one who endures to the end will be saved. When they persecute you in one town, flee to another. I'm speaking the truth: You will not reach all the towns of Israel before the Son of Man returns.

"The disciple is not better than his teacher, nor is a servant above his master. If they call your master 'The Prince of

Demons,' what do you think they'll call you who serve him? Do not be afraid of them. Everything will be revealed—whatever is secret will be made public.

"Whatever I tell you in darkness, shout in the daylight. Whatever you hear me whisper in your ear, preach from the housetops. Don't fear those who kill the body. They are not able to kill the soul. Instead, be afraid of the one who can destroy both the soul and the body in hell.

"Aren't two sparrows sold for a penny? Not one of them will fall to the ground without your Father's knowledge of it. In fact, the hairs on your head are all numbered. Don't be afraid, for you are more valuable than many sparrows.

"Speak of me publicly. Then I will speak of you to my Father who is in heaven. But whoever denies me publicly, I will deny to my Father. Do not think that I have come to bring peace on earth. I have brought a sword! I have come to turn a man against his father, a daughter against her mother, and a daughter-in-law against her mother-in-law. One's enemies will be in his own household.

"If you love your father or mother more than me, you are not worthy to be with me. He that loves his son or daughter more than me is not worthy of me. He that does not take his cross and follow me is not worthy of me. He that finds his life will lose it, and he that loses his life for me will find it.

"Whoever welcomes you welcomes me as well. And he who welcomes me welcomes the Father who sent me. Whoever accepts a prophet for what he is will receive a prophet's reward; he who accepts a righteous man for what he is will receive a righteous man's reward. Whoever gives one of my least important followers a cup of water to drink will not lose his reward."

When Jesus had finished giving this guidance to his twelve disciples, he went away to teach and to preach in Galilee.

Retreating to a Deserted Place

The Death of John

Matt. 14:1-12
Mark 6:14-29
Luke 9:7-9

King Herod heard of Jesus (his name was well known) and swore, "John the Baptist is risen from the dead! So he does these powerful things." Others said, "It is Elijah." Still others said, "He is a prophet, or like one of the prophets." When Herod heard this he said, "It is John, whom I beheaded. He is risen from the dead."

Herod had arrested John, and locked him in prison. Herod did this because he had married Herodias, his brother Philip's wife, and John had told Herod, "It is not lawful for you to have your brother's wife." So Herodias resented him and wanted him killed; but she could not arrange this, because Herod feared John. He knew that he was a just and holy man; he revered John and heard him gladly.

But Herodias found a convenient day when Herod gave a banquet on his birthday for his lords, high captains, and chiefs of Galilee. Herodias's daughter came to the party and danced. This pleased Herod and those who sat with him. The king said to the young woman, "Ask anything of me and I will give it to you." He swore to her, "Whatever you ask of me, I will give it to you, up to half of my kingdom."

She went out and said to her mother, "What should I ask for?" Her mother replied, "The head of John the Baptist." She hurried to the king and said, "I want you to give me the head of John the

Baptist on a platter." The king was very sorry; yet because he had sworn with an oath, and because those who sat with him were watching, he did not refuse her.

Immediately, Herod sent an executioner and commanded John's head to be brought to him. The executioner went and beheaded John in the prison and brought his head on a platter and gave it to the girl and she gave it to her mother. When John's disciples heard the news, they took up his corpse and buried it in a tomb.

Feeding Five
Thousand
in Bethsaida

Matt. 14:13-23
Mark 6:30-44
Luke 9:10-17
John 6:1-15

The apostles gathered together, came to Jesus, and told him what they had done, and what they had taught. He said to them, "Come away to a deserted place with me and rest a while." (There were many people coming and going and they had no time even to eat.)

They departed alone by boat to a deserted place, but the people saw them leave. Many knew where he was going and outran the boat to get there first, because they had seen the miracles he had done for the sick. When Jesus came out of the boat, he saw the crowd and was moved with love for them. They were like sheep without a shepherd. So he taught them many things, and healed their sick.

When the day was almost over, his disciples came to him and said, "This is a deserted place and the day is over. Send them away so that they can go into the countryside and villages and buy food; they have nothing to eat." He answered, "You give them something to eat." They said to him, "Do you want us to spend a small fortune on bread and give it to them to eat?"

He said to them, "Go and see how many loaves of bread you have." They said, "Five loaves and two fish." He told them to have all the people sit down in groups on the green grass. So they sat down in groups of hundreds and fifties.

Jesus took the five loaves and the two fish, looked up to heaven, blessed and broke the loaves, and gave them to his disciples to serve to the people. He divided the two fish among them all. They all ate and were filled, and they gathered twelve baskets full of the leftovers. The number of people who ate were about five thousand men, not including women and children.

Then some men who saw the miracle said, "For sure this is the prophet that will come to the world." When Jesus understood that they wanted to take him by force and make him a king, he went away to a mountain by himself.

Rescuing the
Disciples
*on the Sea
of Galilee*

Matt. 14:22-36
Mark 6:45-56
John 6:16-21

Jesus convinced his disciples to board a boat and go ahead of him to the other side of the lake while he sent away the crowd. When he had sent the crowd away, he went up to a mountain to pray. When evening came, he was there alone.

The boat was in the middle of the lake, tossed with waves because the wind was against it. At three in the morning, Jesus went out to them, walking on the lake. He would have passed by, but when the disciples saw him walking on the lake, they were troubled. "It is a spirit!" they shouted, and cried out in fear.

But Jesus spoke to them, saying, "Relax, it's I. Don't be afraid." Peter answered, "Lord, if it is you, ask me come out to you by walking on the water." Jesus said, "Come on." Peter came out of the boat, and walked on the water to go to Jesus. But when he saw that the wind was wild, he was afraid and began to sink, yelling, "Lord, save me." Jesus reached out, grabbed him, and said, "You have so little faith, why did you doubt?" Then the two men came into the boat and the wind ceased.

Then those in the boat worshipped him, saying, "Truly you are the Son of God." (They had forgotten the miracle of the loaves, because their hearts were hard.)

When they had crossed the lake, they came to the land of Gennesaret. When people there heard he had arrived, they went out into the countryside and brought to him all kinds of sick and diseased people. They begged to touch the hem of his garment, and those who touched it became perfectly healthy.

The next day, the people on the other side of the lake saw that there was no other boat there except the one his disciples used. They knew that Jesus had not gone into the boat with his disciples and that his disciples had gone away alone (even though

Revealing the Bread of Life

True Bread vs. Miracles *in Capernaum*

John 6:22-40

other boats had come from Tiberias, which was near the place where they ate the bread after the Lord had given thanks). When the people saw that Jesus and his disciples were not there, they also took boats to Capernaum, looking for Jesus.

They found him on the other side of the lake, and said to him, "Teacher, when did you come here?" Jesus answered, "Here is the truth: You don't seek me because you saw the miracles, but because you enjoyed eating the bread. Don't work for the food which passes away, but for the food which endures to eternal life. The Son of Man gives this food to you because God the Father sent me for this purpose."

Then they said to him, "How should we do the works of God?" Jesus answered, "This is the work of God, that you believe in him whom he has sent." So they said to him, "What sign will you show us that we may believe you are the one? What will you do? For example, our fathers ate manna in the desert. It is written, 'He gave them bread from heaven to eat.' "

Jesus said, "I'll tell you the truth, Moses did not give you that bread from heaven. My Father gives you the true bread from heaven. The bread of God is the one who comes down from heaven and gives life to the world." Then they said, "Lord, give us this bread forever."

Jesus said to them, "I am the bread of life. Whoever comes to me will never hunger. He who believes in me will never thirst. You have seen me and do not believe. Yet everyone that the Father gives me will come to me; and I will not cast out those who come. I did not come down from heaven to do my own will, but to do the will of him who sent me.

"The Father has sent me and this is his will: That I will lose none of the people he has given me, but will raise them up on the last day. This is the will of him who sent me: All who seek the Son and believe in him will have eternal life, and I will raise them up on the last day."

The Jewish leaders murmured because he said, "I am the bread which came down from heaven." They complained, "Isn't this Jesus, the son of Joseph? We know his father and mother. How can he say, 'I

How to Have an Inner Life

John 6:41-59

came down from heaven?' "

Jesus answered them, "Do not murmur among yourselves. No one can come to me unless the Father attracts him. The prophets wrote, 'And they will all be taught of God.' Every one who has heard, and has learned from the Father, comes to me, and I will raise him up on the last day. Not that anyone has ever seen the Father. The one who is of God has seen the Father. Here's the truth: The person who believes in me has eternal life.

"I am the bread of life. Your fathers ate manna in the wilderness and are dead. This is the bread that comes down from heaven that a person may eat of it and not die. I am the living bread that came down from heaven. If anyone eats this bread, he will live forever. The bread that I will give is my flesh, which I will give for the life of the world." The Jews argued among themselves, "How can this man give us his flesh to eat?"

Then Jesus said to them, "Listen to this truth: Unless you eat the flesh of the Son of Man, and drink his blood, you have no life within yourself. Whoever eats my flesh, and drinks my blood, has eternal life; and I will raise him up on the last day. Because my flesh is real food, and my blood is real drink. He who eats my flesh, and drinks my blood, dwells in me, and I in him.

"The living Father has sent me, and I live because of the Father. In the same way, whoever eats me will live because of me. This is the bread that came down from heaven. It is not the same as the manna your fathers ate. They are dead. He who eats this bread will live forever."

Jesus said these things in the synagogue as he taught in Capernaum.

Many of his disciples, when they heard this, said, "This is a difficult statement; who can understand it?" Jesus was aware that his disciples were murmuring. He said to them, "Does this statement offend you? What if you were to see the Son of Man ascend up to where he was before? It is the Spirit that gives life; my flesh is worthless. The words that I speak to you, they are Spirit, and they are life. But some of you do not believe." (Jesus knew from

It Is the
Spirit that
Gives Life

John 6:60-71

the beginning who did not believe and who would betray him.) He continued, "This is why I said to you that no man can come to me unless my Father attracts him."

From that time, many of his disciples went away and no longer associated with him. Then Jesus said to the twelve apostles, "Will you go away, too?" Simon Peter answered, "Lord, whom should we go to? You have the words of eternal life. We believe and are certain that you are the Christ, the Son of the living God." Jesus answered, "I have chosen you twelve, and one of you is a devil." (He was speaking of Judas Iscariot, the son of Simon, one of the twelve, because he would betray him.)

Then scribes and Pharisees came to Jesus from Jerusalem, asking, "Why do your disciples break our traditions? They do not wash their hands when they eat." He answered them, saying, "Why does your tradition break the commandment of God? God commanded, 'Honor your father and mother'; and 'He who curses his father or mother must die.' But you say, 'A son may tell his parents, "The money which was earmarked for you, I have given to the temple." ' This is not an honor to parents. So you have negated God's commandment by your tradition.

"You hypocrites, Isaiah was right when he prophesied about you: 'This people comes near me with their words, and honors me with their lips; but their heart is far away from me. Their worship is empty and they teach human laws like they were equal to God's commandments.' "

He called to the crowd and said to them, "Listen and try to understand me. That which goes into your mouth does not defile you. Rather it is that which comes out of your mouth that defiles you."

His disciples came and said to him, "Do you know that the Pharisees were offended when they heard you say this?" He answered, "Every plant that has not been planted by my heavenly Father will be uprooted. Let them alone. They are blind leaders of the blind. And if the blind lead the blind, both will fall into the ditch."

Then Peter said to him, "Explain this parable to us."

Jesus said, "Do you still not understand? Don't you know that the food you put in your mouth goes into the belly and is soon flushed down the drain? But those things that come out of the mouth come from your heart. These things defile you. For out of the heart come evil thoughts, murder, adultery, fornication, theft, lies, blasphemy—these are the things that defile you. Eating without washing your hands is not defiling."

CHAPTER FIVE

THE END OF
HIS WORK IN GALILEE

Then Jesus went away to Tyre and Sidon, and stayed in a house there. He wanted no one to know where he was, but he could not be hidden. A Canaanite woman came and cried out to him, "Have mercy on me, O Lord, son of David; my daughter is deranged with a devil."

Jesus did not answer her. His disciples told him, "Send her away; she is shouting at us." He said, "I am only sent to find the lost sheep of the house of Israel."

Then she came and worshipped him: "Lord, help me." But he answered, "It is not right to take the children of Israel's

Retreating Northward

Crumbs for Gentile Dogs in Tyre

Matt. 15:21-28
Mark 7:24-30

bread, and throw it to Gentile dogs." And she said, "This is true, Lord: yet the dogs eat the crumbs that fall from their master's table."

Then Jesus said to her, "O woman, your faith is great! You can have what you want." And her daughter was immediately healed.

The Astonishment of Decapolis *in Decapolis*

Matt. 15: 29-31
Mark 7:31-37

So Jesus left Tyre and Sidon and came to the Sea of Galilee through the middle of Decapolis. They brought to him someone who was deaf and had an impediment in his speech. They begged him to put his hand upon him. Jesus took him away from the crowd and put his fingers into his ears. He spit and touched his tongue. Looking up to heaven, he sighed, and said to him, "Ephphatha"; that is, "Be opened." Right away the man's ears were opened, the string of his tongue was loosed, and he spoke plainly.

Jesus told them to tell no one. But the more he told them this, the more they announced it. They were astonished, saying, "He has done everything well. He makes the deaf hear, and the dumb speak."

In those days, the crowd was huge and had nothing to eat. Jesus called to his disciples and said, "I care about the crowd. They have been with me three days now and have nothing to eat. If I send them back to their own houses hungry, they will faint by the roadside. Many of them came from far away."

His disciples answered, "How can we satisfy these men with bread here in the wilderness?" He asked them, "How many loaves do you have?" They said, "Seven."

He commanded the people to sit down on the ground, took the seven loaves, gave thanks, broke the bread, and gave it to his disciples to give to them. They gave the bread to the people. They also had a few small fish. He blessed these and told them to give them to the people. So they all ate and were satisfied. The disciples collected seven baskets of leftover food. Four thousand men ate, besides women and children. Then he sent away the crowd, took a boat, and came to Magdala.

The Leaven
of Religious
Doctrine
in Magdala

*Matt. 15:39-
16:12*
Mark 8:10-21

The Pharisees and Sadducees came and tempted him to show them a sign from heaven. He said to them, "When it is evening, you say, 'It will be fair weather, the sky in the west is red.' And in the morning, 'It will be foul weather today, the sky in the east is red and lowering.' O you hypocrites, you can read the face of the sky, but not the signs of the times.

"A wicked and adulterous generation wants a sign from heaven. There will be no sign given to them, except the sign of the prophet Jonah." He left them.

When his disciples arrived at the other side of the lake, they had forgotten to bring food. Jesus said to them, "Beware of the leaven of the Pharisees and of the Sadducees." They reasoned among themselves: "He says this because we have no bread." When Jesus understood that they thought this, he said to them, "O you of little faith, why do you reason among yourselves? Is it because you have no bread? Don't you understand yet? Remember the five loaves of the five thousand, and how many basketsful were left over? And the seven loaves of the four thousand,

and how many basketsful were left over?

"How can it be that you don't understand that I wasn't telling you about bread when I said that you should beware of the leaven of the Pharisees and the Sadducees?" They finally understood that he was not telling them to beware of the leaven of bread, but to be careful of the doctrine of the Pharisees and Sadducees.

When he came to Bethsaida, people brought a blind man to Jesus, and begged him to touch him. He took the blind man by the hand and led him out of town. He spit on his eyes, put his hands upon him, and asked him if he could see.

His
Healing
Spit
in Bethsaida

Mark
8:22-26

The man looked up and said, "I see men like trees, except they are walking." After that he put his hands again upon the man's eyes and made him look up. He was restored, and saw everyone clearly. Jesus sent him away, saying, "Do not go into the town, or tell this to anyone there."

When Jesus came into the coasts of Caesarea Philippi, he asked his disciples, "Who do people say that I am?" They

**Retreating
Northward
Again**

The Revelation
that Builds
the Church
*in Caesarea
Philippi*

Matt. 16:13-20
Mark 8:27-30
Luke 9:18-21

answered, "Some say that you are John the Baptist; some say, Elijah; and others, Jeremiah or one of the prophets."

He said to them, "But who do you say that I am?" Simon Peter answered, "You are the Christ, the Son of the living God."

Jesus said to him, "You are blessed, Simon Barjona, because no one has revealed this to you except my Father, who is in heaven. And I tell you: You are Peter, and on this rock I will build my church. The gates of hell will not prevail against it. And I will give you the keys of the kingdom of heaven. Whatever you bind on earth will be bound in heaven; and whatever you will loose on earth will be loosed in heaven."

Then he told his disciples that they should not tell anyone that he was the Christ.

Predicting His
Death and
Resurrection

Matt. 16:21-28
Mark 8:31-9:1
Luke 9:22-27

From that time on, Jesus began to tell his disciples that he had to go to Jerusalem, suffer many things at the hands of the elders, chief priests, and scribes, be killed, and be raised again the third day. But Peter took him aside and began to rebuke him, saying, "Lord, this must not happen to you." But Jesus turned and said to Peter, "Get behind me, Satan, and shut up. You are a stumbling block. You care nothing for the things of God, but prefer human things."

Jesus said to his disciples, "If any man wants to be my follower, he must deny himself, take up his cross, and follow me. For whoever wants to save his life will lose it, and whoever will lose his life for my sake will find it. What is the profit if someone gains the whole world and loses his own soul? What will a man give in exchange for his soul? Because the Son of Man will come in the glory of his Father with his angels. Then he will reward everyone according to his or her works.

"Listen to this: There are some people standing here who will not die until they see the Son of Man coming in his kingdom."

Six days later, Jesus took Peter, James, and John his brother up to a high mountain apart from the others. There he was transfigured in front of them. His face shone

The Revelation of Jesus Alone at Mt. Hermon

Matt. 17:1-13
Mark 9:2-13
Luke 9:28-36

like the sun and his clothing was white as the light. And Moses and Elijah appeared and were talking with Jesus.

Peter said to Jesus, "Lord, it is wonderful to be here. If you want, let's erect three sacred tents: one for you, one for Moses, and one for Elijah." While he spoke, a bright cloud overshadowed them and a voice spoke out of the cloud, "This is my beloved Son in whom I am well pleased; listen to him."

When the disciples heard the voice, they fell on their faces, and were very afraid. Jesus came over, touched them, and said, "Get up, and don't be afraid." When they looked up, they saw no one, except Jesus alone. As they came down from the mountain, Jesus said, "Do not tell anyone about this vision until the Son of Man is risen from the dead."

Next, his disciples asked him, "Why do the scribes say that Elijah must come first? Jesus answered them, "This is true that Elijah will first come and restore all things. But I say to you that Elijah has come already and they did not know it was he. Instead, they did whatever they wanted to him. Likewise, the Son of Man will suffer at their hands." Then the disciples understood that he spoke of John the Baptist.

When he came to his disciples, he saw a big crowd around them and the scribes questioning them. When all the people saw him, they were amazed and ran to greet him. He asked the scribes, "Why are you questioning them?"

One of the crowd answered, "Master, I have brought my son to you. He has a dumb spirit that takes him and tears him. He foams, and gnashes with his teeth, and pines away. I spoke to your disciples and asked them to cast him out and they could not."

Jesus answered, "O faithless generation, how long will I be with you? How long will I endure you? Bring him to me." They brought him, and when the boy saw Jesus, the spirit immediately tore him and he fell on the ground in convulsions, foaming at the mouth. Jesus asked the father, "How long has this been happening to him?" He said, "Since he was a child. Often it has cast him into the fire,

Displaying Faith to a Faithless Generation *near Mt. Hermon*

Matt. 17:14-20
Mark 9:14-29
Luke 9:37-43

and into the water, trying to destroy him. If you can do anything, have compassion, and help us."

Jesus said to him, "If you can believe, all things are possible." Immediately the father of the child cried out, with tears, "Lord, I believe; please help my unbelief!" When Jesus saw that the people came running together, he rebuked the foul spirit, "You dumb and deaf spirit, I command that you come out of him, and never come back."

The spirit cried, tore the boy, and came out of him. The boy seemed to be dead. In fact, many said, "He is dead." But Jesus took him by the hand, lifted him, and he got up.

When Jesus came into the house, his disciples asked him privately, "Why couldn't we cast the devil out?" He said to them, "Because of your unbelief. Here's what I have to say to you: If you have faith the size of a mustard seed, you will be able to say to this mountain, 'Move over there' and it will move. Nothing will be impossible for you. This kind of demon will come out only by prayer and fasting."

They departed and traveled through Galilee. But Jesus did not want anyone to know it, because he was teaching his disciples: "The Son of Man will be delivered into human hands, they will kill him, and after he is killed, he will rise the third day." But they didn't understand what he was talking about, and were afraid to ask him about it.

Predicting His Death and Resurrection Again

Matt. 17:22-23
Mark 9:30-32
Luke 9:43-45

When they came to Capernaum, the tax collectors came to Peter and said, "Doesn't your master pay the temple tax?" Peter answered, "Yes."

Returning to Galilee

Does God Pay the Temple Tax?
in Capernaum

Matt. 17:24-27

When he came back to the house, Jesus asked him, "What do you think, Simon? From whom do kings collect their taxes—their own children or from strangers?" Peter said to him, "From strangers." Jesus said to him, "Then the children are free from taxes."

"Nevertheless, just so we don't offend them, go to the lake, cast in a hook, and take the first fish that comes up. When you open its mouth, you will find a coin. Take that and give it to the tax collectors for me and you."

Instructions on
the Kingdom

• Who Is the
Greatest?

Matt. 18:1-6
Mark 9:33-42
Luke 9:46-50

In the house he asked them, "What was it that you were disputing about along the road?" They held their peace because they had disputed about who would be the greatest among them.

He sat down and said to them, "Anyone who wants to be first will be the last of all, and servant of all." At the same time, the disciples asked Jesus, "Then who is the greatest in the kingdom of heaven?"

Jesus called to a little child, set him in front of them, and said, "Unless you become like little children, you will not enter into the kingdom of heaven. Whoever humbles himself like this little child is greatest in the kingdom of heaven."

Then John said, "Master, we saw someone casting out devils in your name. We told him to stop because he doesn't follow us."

Jesus said, "Don't do that. No man can do a miracle in my name and lightly speak evil about me. He that is not against us is for us. Whoever will give you a cup of water to drink because you belong to me, I say to you, he will not lose his reward. And whoever will offend one of these little ones who believe in me, it would be better for him if a millstone were hung on his neck, and he were thrown into the sea.

Woe to the world because of offenses! For offenses must come; but woe to that man who brings them!

• The Offense of Despising Others

Matt. 18:7-14
Mark 9:43-50

"If your hand offends you, cut it off. It is better for you to enter into life maimed, than to go into hell with two hands— where the worm does not die, and the fire is not put out. If your foot offends you, cut it off. It is better for you to enter lame into life, than to be cast into hell with two feet —where the worm does not die, and the fire is not put out. And if your eye offends you, pluck it out. It is better for you to enter into the kingdom of God with one eye, than to be cast into hell fire with two eyes—where the worm does not die, and the fire is not put out. Every one will be salted with fire, and every sacrifice will be salted with salt. Salt is good, but if the salt has lost its saltiness, what good is it? Have salt for yourself, and have peace with one another.

"Be careful not to despise one of these

little ones. I tell you, in heaven their angels always behold the face of my Father. For the Son of Man has come to save that which was lost.

"What do you think—if a man has a hundred sheep, and one of them wanders away, doesn't he leave the ninety-nine, go into the mountains, and seek the one that has gone astray? If he finds it, I tell you, he rejoices more about that sheep than over the ninety-nine that did not wander. Your Father in heaven does not want one of these little ones to perish.

• How to Care for Others

Matt. 18:15-35

Not only so, if your brother trespasses against you, go and tell him about it privately. If he listens to you, you have gained your brother. But if he doesn't hear you, take one or two others with you so that they can witness what he says to you. And if he neglects to listen to them, tell it to the church. But if he neglects to hear the church, let him be like a heathen and a publican to you.

"I want you to know that whatever you bind on earth will be bound in heaven: and whatever you loose on earth will be loosed in heaven. Also, if two of you will agree on earth concerning anything that you ask, it will be done by my Father in heaven. Because where two or three are gathered together in my name, I am there among them."

Then Peter came to him and said, "Lord, how often can my brother sin against me and I should forgive him? Seven times?" Jesus said to him, "Not seven times: but, seventy times seven.

"You see, the kingdom of heaven is like a king settling the accounts of his servants. He began reckoning and one was brought to him who owed him millions. Since the servant had nothing to pay, the king commanded that he be sold, together with his wife, and children, and all his possessions, so that payment could be made.

"The servant fell down and worshipped him, saying, 'Lord, have patience with me and I will pay you everything.' Then the king had pity, freed him, and forgave him the debt. But then the servant went out and found another servant who owed him a few thousand dollars, took him by the throat, and said, 'Pay me what you owe.' This servant fell down at his feet and begged, 'Have patience with me, and I will pay you everything.' But he would not do this. Instead he went and cast him into prison till he could pay the debt.

"When the other servants saw what had happened, they were very sorry and came and told their lord all that had been done. Then his lord called him and said, 'You wicked servant, I forgave you all that debt, simply because you asked me to. Shouldn't you have had compassion on your fellow servant just like I had pity on you?'

"His lord was angry and sent him to the jailers till he could pay all he owed. My heavenly Father will do this to you if, from your hearts, you do not forgive others."

Visiting Jerusalem

The Ridicule of His Family *in Capernaum*

John 7:1-9

After this, Jesus lived in Galilee. He wouldn't live among the Jews, because they wanted to kill him.

But a feast of the Jews, the Feast of Tabernacles, was coming up and Jesus' brothers said to him, "Leave here. Go to Judea, so that your disciples can see the miracles you do. No one works in secret who wants to be known. Since you do all these things, go show yourself to the rest of world." (His brothers did not believe in him.)

Jesus said to them, "It is not the right time for this, but you can go at any time. The world cannot hate you, but it hates me, because I reveal its sin and evil works. You go on up to the feast. I won't go yet. The time is not right." So he stayed in Galilee.

But when his brothers were gone, he went to the feast (not openly, but in secret). The Jewish leaders looked for him there. "Where is he?" they asked. And the people murmured about him. Some said, "He is a good man." Others said, "No, he deceives people." However, no one spoke about him openly, for fear of the Jewish leaders.

About halfway through the feast, Jesus went into the temple and taught. The Jewish leaders marveled, "How does this man know so much? He never studied like we have." Jesus answered, "My teaching is not my own. It belongs to him who sent me. Anyone who does God's will knows

The Marvel of His Teaching *in Jerusalem*

John 7:10-31

whether this teaching is of God, or if I speak my own ideas. He who teaches his own ideas seeks his own glory. But he who seeks the glory of him who sent him is true, and no unrighteousness is in him.

"Didn't Moses give you the law? Yet none of you keeps the law. Why do you want to kill me?" The people answered, "You have a devil. Who wants to kill you?" Jesus said to them, "I healed one man on the Sabbath, and you all marvel. Yet Moses gave you the way of circumcision (though it is not of Moses, but of the ancient fathers), and you are willing to circumcise a man on the Sabbath. If a man receives circumcision on the Sabbath, so that the law of Moses will not be broken, why are you angry at me because I have healed a man on the Sabbath? Do not judge according to appearance, but judge according to righteousness."

Then some from Jerusalem said, "Isn't this the man they want to kill? Look how boldly he speaks, yet they say nothing to him. Do the rulers think that he is the Christ? How can he be? We know where this man comes from. But when Christ comes, no one knows where he comes from." Then Jesus shouted in the temple where he was teaching, "You know me, and you know where I come from. But I do not represent myself; he who sent me is true (whom you do not know). But I know him, because I am from him, and he has sent me."

Then they looked for a way to arrest him, but no one actually tried, because the time was not right. And many of the people believed in him, and said, "When Christ comes, will he do more miracles than this man?"

Every one went to his own house, but Jesus went to the Mount of Olives. Early in the morning, he came to the temple again, and all the people came to him. He sat down and taught them. Then the scribes and Pharisees brought a woman to him who had been caught in the act of adultery. They stood her in front of him and said, "Master, this woman was caught in adultery, in the very act. Now Moses, in the law, commanded that such a person should be stoned. What do you say?"

The Religious Leaders Lay a Trap

John 7:53-8:11

(They were tempting him so that they could accuse him of disagreeing with the law of Moses.) Jesus stooped down, and with his finger wrote on the ground. It was as though he did not hear. When they continued asking him about this, he stood up and said, "Whoever among you is without sin, let him cast the first stone at her." Again he stooped down and wrote on the ground.

Those who heard what he said were convicted by their own consciences and went out one by one, beginning with the oldest, until they all were gone. Jesus was left alone with the woman standing in the middle of it all. When Jesus stood up and saw no one but the woman, he said to her, "Woman, where are those who accuse you? Hasn't anyone condemned you?" She said, "No one, Lord." Jesus said to her, "I don't condemn you either; go, and sin no more."

Speaking the Words of His Father

John 8:12-30

Then Jesus spoke to them again: "I am the light of the world. Whoever follows me will not live in darkness, but will have the light of life."

The Pharisees then said to him, "You

are making false claims about yourself."

Jesus said to them, "I am talking about myself, but what I say is true. I know where I came from and where I am going; but you know neither of these things. You judge me only by what you can see on the surface. I judge no one. Yet if I do judge, my judgment is true. Why? Because I am not alone, I am with the Father who sent me. It is written in your law that if two people testify the same, what they testify is true—I testify about myself, and the Father who sent me testifies for me as well."

Then they said to him, "Where is your Father?" Jesus answered, "You do not know me, or my Father. If you knew who I am, you would also know my Father." When Jesus said these things he was teaching in the temple treasury, and no one tried to arrest him because the time was not yet right.

Then Jesus said to them, "I am going away, and you will seek me, but you will die in your sins. You cannot come where I am going." Then the Jewish leaders said, "Is he going to kill himself? What does he mean, 'You cannot come where I am going?' " He said to them, "You are from below; I am from above. You are of this world; I am not of this world. Here is why I said that you will die in your sins: If you do not believe that I am who I say I am, you will die in your sins."

Then they said to him, "Who are you?" Jesus said, "I have told you who I am from the beginning. I have not changed. I have many things to say and to judge about you. But the one who has sent me is true and I speak to the world the things that I have heard from him." But they did not understand that he was speaking to them about the Father.

Next Jesus said to them, "When you have lifted up the Son of Man, you will realize who I am and that I have done nothing alone. Rather, I speak the things my Father has taught me. He who sent me is with me—the Father has not left me alone, because I always do what pleases him." And many people believed in him as he spoke these things.

Telling the Liberating Truth

John 8:31-47

Jesus spoke to the Jews who believed in him: "If you live according to my teachings, then you are really my disciples; and you will know the truth, and the truth will make you free."

Others answered, "We are Abraham's descendants, and have never been slaves to anyone. How can you say that we will be made free?" Jesus answered, "I'll tell you: Whoever sins is the slave of sin. And a slave is not a part of the family. Only a son or daughter is always part of the family. If the Son sets you free, you will truly be free. I know that you are Abraham's descendants, but some of you want to kill me. Why? Because my message has no place in your hearts. I am telling you what I saw when I was with my Father. Yet you do what your own father tells you to do."

They answered him: "Abraham is our father." Jesus said, "If you were Abraham's children, you would follow his example. Instead you want to kill me—and for what? All I've done is tell you the truth I have heard from God. Abraham would not kill me for this. Therefore, you are obeying your real father." Then they said to him, "We were not conceived in fornication; we have one Father—God!"

Jesus said to them, "If God were your Father, you would love me, because I came to you from God. It was not my idea to come. He sent me. Why do you not understand what I say to you? You cannot understand me, because you are of your father the devil, and you do what your father wants you to do. He was a murderer from the beginning, and hates the truth, because there is no truth in him. When he lies, he does what comes naturally, because he is a liar, and the father of lies. I, on the other hand, tell you the truth, but you do not believe me.

"Which of you accuses me of sin? And if I tell the truth, why don't you believe me? God's children hear God's words. You cannot hear them, because you are not God's children."

Revealing His Eternal Nature

John 8:48-59

The Jewish leaders said, "We were right, you are a Samaritan, and you have a devil!"

Jesus answered, "I don't have a devil. I honor my Father, and you dishonor me. I am not looking for glory for myself. God is the judge of this. But I say to you, if a man does what I say, he will never see death."

Then they said to him, "Now we know for sure that you have a devil! Abraham is dead, and so are the prophets. Yet you say, 'If a man does what I say, he will never see death.' Are you greater than our father Abraham, who is dead? Or the prophets, who are also dead? Who do you think you are?"

Jesus answered, "If I honor myself, it means nothing. My Father is the one who honors me. You say that he is your God, yet you do not know him; but I know him. And if I were to say, 'I don't know him,' I would be a liar like you. But I do know him, and I obey him. Your father Abraham looked forward to my coming. When he saw it, he was glad."

The Jewish leaders said to him, "You are not even fifty years old! Have you seen Abraham?" Jesus said, "Before Abraham was born, I existed." Then they took stones to throw at him. But Jesus hid from them and went out of the temple.

CHAPTER SIX

HIS FINAL TRIP
TO JERUSALEM

Jesus left Galilee to travel into Judea along the far side of the Jordan River. The people came to him again, and, as he was accustomed, he taught them. When the time came for him to return to God, he faithfully turned to go to Jerusalem. And he sent messengers ahead. They entered into a Samaritan village to make arrangements for him, but the village did not receive him, because they could tell he was going on to Jerusalem.

When his disciples James and John saw this, they said, "Lord, do you want us

Setting the Standard of Discipleship
on the road to Jerusalem

Matt. 19:1-2;
8:18-22
Mark 10:1
Luke 9:51-62

to command fire to come down from heaven and burn them up, just like Elijah did?" He rebuked them, saying, "You don't know what kind of spirit you have. The Son of Man didn't come to destroy lives, but to save them." So they went to another village.

And it so happened that as they went along the road, a man said to Jesus, "Lord, I will follow you wherever you go." Jesus said to him, "Foxes have holes, and birds have nests, but the Son of Man has nowhere to lay his head." He said to another man, "Follow me." But the man said, "Lord, allow me first to go and bury my father." Jesus said to him, "Let the dead bury their dead. You go and preach the kingdom of God. Another said, "Lord, I will follow you, but let me first go bid farewell to those who are at my house." And Jesus said to him, "A man who puts his hand to the plow and then looks back is not qualified for the kingdom of God."

Sending Out Seventy Messengers
at Galilee and Samaria

Luke 10:1-16

After this, the Lord appointed seventy other disciples and sent them two by two ahead of him to every place on his itinerary. He told them, "The harvest is big, but the laborers are few. Pray to the Lord of the harvest that he would send laborers into his harvest. Go your way— but look, I send you like lambs among wolves. Do not carry a purse, cash, or shoes, and pause to greet no one by the road. Whatever house you enter, first say, 'Peace to this house.' If a child of peace is there, your greeting will be received. If not, it will return to you. Stay in that house, eat and drink what they give you. The worker deserves to be paid. But do not go house to house.

"When you enter a town, and they welcome you, eat what is set before you. Heal the sick that are there, and say to them, 'The kingdom of God has come near you.' But whatever town does not welcome you, go your way, and say, 'We shake off the dust of your town that clings to us. Nevertheless, be sure of this, the kingdom of God has come near you.' I say that it will be more tolerable for Sodom in the day of judgment, than for that town.

"Woe to you, Chorazin! woe to you, Bethsaida! If the mighty works that have been done in you had been done in Tyre and Sidon, they would have repented a great while ago, sitting in sackcloth and ashes. But it will be more tolerable for Tyre and Sidon at the judgment than for you. And you, Capernaum, which is exalted to heaven, will be thrust down to hell.

"He that hears you hears me; and he that despises you despises me; and he that despises me despises him that sent me."

Blessing the Seventy

Luke 10:17-24

The seventy returned with joy, saying, "Lord, even the devils obey us in your name." And he said to them, "I saw Satan fall from heaven like lightning. Look, I give you power to tread on serpents and scorpions, and power over the enemy. Nothing will hurt you. Yet do not rejoice that the spirits are subject to you. Rather, rejoice because your names are written in heaven."

Then Jesus rejoiced in the Holy Spirit, and said, "I thank you, O Father, Lord of heaven and earth, that you have hid these things from the wise and prudent, and have revealed them to babes. Father, it seemed good to you. All things have been given to me by my Father. No one knows who the Son is except the Father; or who the Father is, except the Son and the person to whom the Son will reveal him."

He turned to his disciples and said privately, "Blessed are the eyes that see the things you see. For I tell you, many prophets and kings have wanted to see the things you see, and have not seen them; and to hear the things you hear, and have not heard them."

A lawyer stood up to test Jesus, saying, "Master, what should I do to inherit eternal life?" Jesus said to him, "What is written in the law?"

He answered, "You must love the Lord your God with all your heart, and with all your soul, and with all your strength, and with all your mind; and love your neighbor as yourself." And Jesus said to him, "You have answered right. Do this and you will live." But the lawyer, trying to defend himself, said to Jesus, "Who is my neighbor?"

Jesus answered: "A man went down from Jerusalem to Jericho. He fell among thieves, who stripped him of his clothes, wounded him, and departed, leaving him half dead. By chance, a priest came down

The Evidence of Eternal Life

Love:
The Good Samaritan

Luke 10:25-37

that way. When he saw him, he passed by on the other side of the road. In the same way, a Levite came to the place, looked at him, and passed by on the other side. But a Samaritan journeyed to where the wounded man lay. When he saw him, he cared about him, went to him, bandaged his wounds, pouring in oil and wine, put him on his own donkey, brought him to an inn, and took care of him. The next day, when the Samaritan left, he gave two pieces of silver to the host of the inn, and said, 'Take care of him. Whatever you spend more than this, I will repay you when I come again.'

"Which of these three men do you think was a neighbor to the man who fell among the thieves?" The lawyer said, "The one who showed mercy on him." Jesus said to him, "You go, and do the same."

Resting, Not Working: Mary and Martha in Bethany

Luke 10:38-42

As they traveled, it happened that he entered a village, and a woman named Martha received him into her home. She had a sister called Mary, who sat at Jesus' feet and listened to him. But Martha was worried about the details of serving him. She came to him and said, "Lord, don't you care that my sister has left me to serve alone? Tell her to help me." Jesus answered her, "Martha, Martha, you are careful and troubled about so many things. But only one thing is really necessary, and Mary has chosen that good part, which will not be taken away from her."

As Jesus passed by, he saw a man who had been born blind. His disciples asked him, "Master, who sinned, this man, or his parents, so that he was born blind?" Jesus answered, "Neither this man sinned, nor his parents; but the works of God will be made manifest in him. I must work the works of him who sent me, while it is day. The night comes, when no one can work. As long as I am in the world, I am the light of the world."

When he had spoken this, he spat on the ground, made clay of the spittle, anointed the eyes of the blind man with the clay, and said to him, "Go, wash in the pool of Siloam" (which means "sent"). The man went there, washed, and when

Stopping by Jerusalem

Encountering Spiritual Blindness in Jerusalem

John 9:1-41

he came back he was able to see.

The blind man's neighbors and the people who knew that he had been blind, said, "Isn't this the man who sat and begged?" Some said, "This is he." Others said, "He looks like him." And the man himself said, "I am he." So they said to him, "How were your eyes opened?" He answered, "A man called Jesus made clay, and anointed my eyes, and said to me, 'Go to the pool of Siloam, and wash.' I went, washed, and I received my sight." Then said they to him, "Where is he?" He said, "I don't know."

They brought him to the Pharisees. (It was the Sabbath day when Jesus made the clay, and opened his eyes.) The Pharisees also asked him how he had received his sight. He said to them, "He put clay on my eyes, I washed, and now I see."

Therefore, some of the Pharisees said, "This man Jesus is not of God. He doesn't keep the Sabbath." Others said, "How can a man that is a sinner do such miracles?" And there was a disagreement among them. They asked the blind man, "What do you say about the man who has opened your eyes?" He said, "He is a prophet."

But the Jewish leaders did not believe that he had been blind and received his sight. So they called the parents of the man who had received his sight and asked them, "Is this your son, who you say was born blind? How is it that he now can see?" His parents answered them, "We know that this is our son, and that he was born blind. But why he can now see, we don't know; nor do we know who has opened his eyes. He is of age; ask him. He will speak for himself."

His parents spoke this way because they feared the Jewish leaders. They knew that the leaders had agreed already that anyone who said that Jesus was Christ would be thrown out of the synagogue.

They again called the man who had been blind and said to him, "Give God the credit. We know that this man Jesus is a sinner." He answered and said, "Whether he is a sinner or not, I do not know. One thing I do know: Once I was blind and now I see." Then they said to him again, "What did he do to you? How did he open your eyes?" He answered them, "I have told you already, and you did not listen. Why do you want to hear it again? Do you want to become his disciples?" Then they scorned him and said, "You are his disciple; but we are Moses' disciples. We know that God spoke to Moses. As for this fellow, we don't know where he is from."

The man answered them, "Why, this is amazing! You don't know where he comes from, and yet he has given me my sight. We know that God does not hear sinners. But if a person worships God and does his will, God will hear him. Since the world began, has anyone given sight to someone who was born blind? If this man were not of God, he could do nothing."

They said to him, "You were born entirely in sin, and do you teach us?" They ejected him from the synagogue. Jesus heard that they had thrown him out, found him, and said. "Do you believe in the Son of God?" The man answered, "Who is he, Lord, that I may believe in him?" Jesus said to him, "You have seen him. He is talking with you right now." And the man said, "Lord, I believe." And he worshipped him.

And Jesus said, "I have come into this world for judgment—that they who cannot see might see; and that they who see might be made blind." Some of the Pharisees, who were with him, heard these words and said to him, "Are we blind also?" Jesus said to them, "If you were blind, you would have no sin. But now you say, 'We see.' Therefore your sin remains.

I say to you, the person who does not enter by the door into the sheep barn, but instead climbs in some other way, is a thief and a robber. But he who enters in by the door is the shepherd of the sheep. The doorkeeper opens to him and the sheep hear his voice. He calls his own sheep by name, and leads them out. And when he puts out his own sheep, he goes ahead of them, and the sheep follow him because they know his voice. They will not follow a stranger, but will flee from him. They do not know the voice of strangers." Jesus told this parable, but the Jewish leaders did not understand what he was saying.

Then Jesus said to them, "I am the door for the sheep. All that came before me are

The Parable of the Shepherd and the Thief

John 10:1-21

thieves and robbers; but the sheep did not hear them. I am the door. If any man enters in by me, he will be saved, and will go in and out and find pasture. The thief only comes to steal, to kill, and to destroy. I have come that they may have life, and that they may have it abundantly.

"I am the good shepherd. The good shepherd gives his life for the sheep. But a hired hand sees the wolf coming, leaves the sheep, and runs. So the wolf catches the sheep and scatters them. The hired hand flees because he is a hired hand, and does not care for the sheep. I am the good shepherd and know my sheep, and am known by my sheep. The Father knows me and I know the Father, and I lay down my life for the sheep.

"I have other sheep which are not of this fold. I must bring them in also, and they will hear my voice. There will be one fold and one shepherd. This is why my Father loves me: I lay down my life that I might take it up again. No man takes it from me, but I lay it down by myself. I have power to lay it down and I have power to take it back again. I have received this commandment from my Father."

Then there was a division among the Jewish leaders because of what Jesus said. Many of them said, "He has a devil, and is mad; why do you listen to him?" Others said, "These are not the words of a man who has a devil. Can a devil open the eyes of the blind?"

Jesus answered them, "I have shown you many of my Father's good works; for which of those works do you want to stone me to death?" The Jewish leaders answered, "We don't stone you for a good work, but for blasphemy. You are a man, but you make yourself God."

Jesus answered them, "Isn't it written in your law, 'I said, you are gods?' He called those to whom this word came, 'gods,' and the Scripture cannot be broken. The Father has made me holy, and sent me into the world, yet you say to me 'You blaspheme'; all because I said, 'I am the Son of God.' If I do not do my Father's works, then don't believe me. But if I do, even though you don't believe in me, believe the works. Then you will

Retreating from Danger *west of the Jordan River*

John 10:32-42

know and believe that the Father is in me, and I in him."

Therefore, they tried again to arrest him, but he escaped and went away beyond the Jordan to the place where John first baptized. And he stayed there. Many people came to him there and said, "John did not do even one miracle, but all things that John spoke of this man were true." And many believed in Jesus.

Describing Life in the Kingdom

Praying: the Stone, the Serpent, and the Egg

Luke 11:1-13

Jesus was praying. When he was finished, one of his disciples said, "Lord, teach us to pray like John taught his disciples." And he said to them, "When you pray, say, 'Our Father in heaven, may your name be holy; your kingdom come, and your will be done on earth as it is in heaven. Give us food, day by day. Forgive us our sins; for we also forgive every one who sins against us. And don't lead us into temptation; instead, deliver us from evil.'

"Suppose you go to a friend at midnight and say to him, 'Friend, lend me three loaves of bread. I have a house guest and I have no food to serve him.' From within the house the friend answers,

'Don't trouble me. The door is shut and my children are with me in bed; I cannot get up and give you any bread.' He will not rise out of bed and give you any bread simply because you are his friend. But, because of your persistence, he will rise and give you as many loaves as you need.

"Ask, and it will be given you; seek, and you will find; knock, and it will be opened to you. Because every one who asks, receives; and he who seeks, finds; and to him who knocks it will be opened. If your son asks one of you fathers for bread, will you give him a stone? Or if he asks for a fish, instead of a fish will you give him a serpent? Or if he asks for an egg, will you offer him a scorpion? You are evil, yet you know how to give good gifts to your children. How much more then does your heavenly Father know to give the Holy Spirit to those who ask him?"

Jesus was casting out a devil that could not speak. And it came to pass when the devil was gone out, the dumb person spoke and the people wondered. But some of them said, "He casts out devils through

Hearing the Word of God: the Sign of Jonah

Luke 11:14-32

Beelzebub, the chief of the devils." And others tempted him by asking for a sign from heaven.

But he knew their thoughts, and said to them, "Every kingdom divided against itself is destroyed; and a divided household falls. If Satan is divided against himself, how will his kingdom stand? You say that I cast out devils through Beelzebub. If this is true, by whom do your sons cast them out? Let them be your judges. But if I with the finger of God cast out devils, no doubt the kingdom of God is come to you.

"When a strong man, fully armed, guards his palace, his goods are safe. But when a stronger man comes upon him, and overcomes him, he takes away the weapons in which the strong man trusted, and divides his plunder. He who is not with me is against me; and he who does not gather with me, scatters.

"When an unclean spirit is gone out of a man, it walks through dry places, seeking rest. Finding none, it says, 'I will return to the house where I came from.' And when it comes back, it finds it swept and orderly. Then the unclean spirit finds seven other spirits more wicked than itself. They also enter into the man, and dwell there; and the last state of that man is worse than the first."

As he spoke these things, a woman in the crowd lifted up her voice and said to him, "Blessed is the womb that bore you, and the breasts that nursed you." But he said, "Rather, blessed are they that hear the word of God, and keep it."

And when the people were gathered thick together, he said, "This is an evil generation, because they seek a sign. No sign will be given to it except the sign of Jonah the prophet:

"Just as Jonah was a sign to the Ninevites, so will the Son of Man be a sign to this generation. The queen of the south will rise up in the judgment with this generation, and condemn them. She came from far away to hear the wisdom of Solomon; and look, one greater than Solomon is here. The men of Nineveh will rise up in the judgment with this generation and will condemn it. They repented at the preaching of Jonah; and look, one greater than Jonah is here.

When a man lights a candle he doesn't put it in a secret place, or under a basket, but he puts it on a candlestick, so that they who come into his house may see the light. The light of the body is the eye; therefore, when your eye is single, your whole body is full of light; but when your eye is evil, your body also is full of darkness.

"Be careful that the light that is in you is not darkness. If your whole body is full of light, with no part dark, it will be as full of light as when a bright shining candle gives light."

As he spoke, a Pharisee asked him to dine with him. So Jesus went in, and sat down to eat. When the Pharisee saw this, he marveled that Jesus had not first washed his hands before dinner. The Lord said to him, "You Pharisees make the outside of the cup and the platter clean, but your inward part is full of gluttony and wickedness. You fools, didn't the one who made the outside make the inside too? Give of the things that are within you, and all things will be clean to you.

"But woe to you, Pharisees! You tithe mint and rue and all kinds of herbs, and forget about justice and the love of God. You should have taken care of these without leaving the others undone. Woe to you, Pharisees! You love the honored seats in the synagogues, and the greetings in the markets. Woe to you, scribes and Pharisees, hypocrites! You are like unmarked graves: people walk over you unaware."

Then one of the lawyers answered him, "Master, when you say these things, you insult us also." And Jesus said, "Woe to you also, you lawyers! You load people with burdens which are hard to bear, and you yourselves won't touch these burdens with even one finger. Woe to you! You build the tombs of the prophets whom your ancestors killed. You witness and approve of your ancestors' deeds: they killed the prophets and you build their tombs.

"This is why God in his wisdom said, 'I will send them prophets and apostles. Some of them will be killed and persecuted.' Therefore, this generation is responsible for the blood of all the prophets that has been shed since the world began —from the blood of Abel to the blood of Zechariah, who perished between the altar and the sanctuary. I tell you, this has all been entered against the account of your generation. Woe to you, lawyers! You have taken away the key of knowledge; you did not enter the kingdom yourselves and you hindered those who were entering."

As he said these things to them, the scribes and the Pharisees were very hostile to him and quizzed him about many things, waiting for him to say something wrong so that they could legally accuse him.

The Value of
Human Life

Luke 12:1-12

In the meantime, innumerable people gathered together—so many that they pushed and shoved against each other. Jesus said to his disciples, "Beware of the leaven of the Pharisees, which is hypocrisy. For there is nothing covered that will not be revealed; nothing hidden that will not be known. Therefore, whatever you have spoken in darkness will be heard in the light; and that which you have whispered in closets will be proclaimed upon the housetops.

"I say to you my friends, do not be afraid of those who kill the body. After that there is no more they can do. I will forewarn you about whom to fear: Fear him, who after he has killed, has the power to cast you into hell. Yes, I say to you, fear him.

"Are not five sparrows sold for two cents? Not one of them is forgotten by God. Even the hairs of your head are all numbered. So do not fear, you are of more value than many sparrows.

"Also I say, whoever acknowledges me publicly, I will acknowledge before the angels of God. But he that denies me publicly will be denied before God's angels. If someone speaks a word against the Son of Man, it will be forgiven. But blasphemy against the Holy Spirit will not be forgiven.

"When they bring you to the synagogues, to magistrates and authorities, don't worry about how you will answer them, or what you will say. The Holy Spirit will teach you in that very hour what you should say."

And one of the crowd said to him, "Master, speak to my brother, tell him to divide the inheritance with me." He said

The Value of Material Possessions

Luke 12:13-21

to the man, "Who made me a judge or a arbitrator over you?" And he said to them all, "Beware of covetousness. A man's life does not consist of the abundance of his possessions."

And he told them this parable: "A rich man's land was very fruitful. So he thought, 'What should I do? I have no room to store my crops. Aha! Here's what I'll do: I'll pull down my old barns, and build bigger ones in which to store my crops and my property. Then I can say to myself—You have food and possessions stored up for many years. Take it easy, eat, drink, and be merry.'

"But God said to him, 'You fool, tonight I will demand your life of you. Then who will own the things you have hoarded?' This is the way it is with those who store up treasures for themselves and are not rich toward God."

The True
Treasure

Luke 12:22-34

Jesus said to his disciples, "Do not worry about your life; about what you will eat. Do not worry about your body; about what you will wear. Your life is more than food, and your body is more than clothing. Think of the ravens, they don't sow seed or reap harvests. They don't have storehouses or barns. God feeds them. How much more valuable are you than the birds!

"Can any of you add an hour to your life through worry? If you cannot do that little thing, why do you worry about all the rest of it? Think of how lilies grow. They don't work, they don't spin cloth; and yet Solomon in all his glory was not clothed like one of these lilies. So, since God clothes the grass, which can be seen today in the field, yet tomorrow is burned, don't you think he'll clothe you? O you of little faith!

"Do not worry about what you will eat or what you will drink. Don't have a worried mind. The people of all the nations in the world seek after these things. Your Father knows that you need these things. Instead, seek the kingdom of God. All these things will be given to you as well. Fear not, little flock; it is your Father's good pleasure to give you the kingdom.

"Sell your possessions and give to the poor. In this way you make yourselves purses that do not wear out; you make an investment in heaven that will not fail. No thief can get near it and nothing can corrupt it. For where your treasure is, there your heart will be also."

Responsibility to God

Luke 12:35-48

Turn on your lights and dress for the time to come. Be like people who wait for their master to return from his wedding. When he comes and knocks, they open the door to him immediately. Blessed are the servants whom the master finds waiting and watching when he comes. The master himself will put on an apron, make them sit down for a meal, and will serve them. If he comes late at night or early in the morning and finds them waiting, such servants are blessed.

"Understand this: If the owner of the house had known when the thief would come, he would have been alert and would not have allowed his house to be invaded. Therefore, be ready, because the Son of Man will come at an unexpected time."

Then Peter said to him, "Lord, are you speaking this parable to us, or to all the people?" The Lord said, "Who will be the faithful and wise manager, whom his master will give charge over the people of his household, to give them their food at the proper time? It is that blessed servant who is doing this when his master comes. I tell you the truth, the master will make that servant ruler over all that he has.

"But if that servant says in his heart, 'My lord is slow in coming back,' and so begins to beat the servants and maids, to eat and drink, and to be drunken; that servant's master will come in a day when he is not looking for him—at an hour when he is not aware. The master will cut him in pieces and will cast him out with the faithless.

"The servant who knew what his master wanted, and did not prepare himself, and did not do what his master wanted, will be severely beaten. But the servant who did not know what the master wanted, and did things worthy of a beating, will be lightly punished. To whomever much is given, much is required. People expect much of those they trust.

I came to bring fire on the earth, and I wish it were already kindled! But I have a baptism with which I must be baptized, and am so anxious that it be accomplished! Do you think that I came to give peace on earth? I tell you, no—rather division. From now on, if there are five people in one house, they will be divided three against two, and two against three. The father will be divided against the son, and the son against the father; the mother against the daughter, and the daughter against the mother; the mother-in-law against her daughter-in-law, and the daughter-in-law against her mother-in-law."

He also said to the people, "When you see a cloud rise out of the west, you say, 'Here comes a rain shower,' and it is true. When you feel the south wind blow, you say, 'There will be heat,' and it happens as you say. You hypocrites! You can read the appearance of the sky and the earth, why can't you interpret the present time?

"Why don't you judge for yourselves what is right? When you go to court with your accuser, try your best to settle the case on the way. Otherwise, he could accuse you to the judge, and the judge deliver you to an officer, and the officer throw you into prison. I tell you, you will never get out until you have paid the very last penny."

The Fruit of Repentance

Luke 13:1-9

At that time, some people told him about the Galileans whose blood Pilate had mingled with their sacrifices. Jesus said to them, "Do you think that, because they suffered these things, these Galileans were more sinful than all other Galileans? No. But I tell you, unless you repent, you will all perish like this. What about those eighteen people who were killed when the tower in Siloam fell? Do you think they were greater sinners than everyone else living in Jerusalem? I tell you, no. Unless you repent, you will all perish like this."

He also spoke this parable: "A certain man had a fig tree growing in his vineyard. He came looking for fruit on it, and found none. Then he said to the keeper of his vineyard, 'For three years I've come looking for fruit on this fig tree, and have found none. Cut it down! Why should it take space in the vineyard?' The keeper said to him, 'Master, let it alone this year, until I cultivate and fertilize it. If it bears fruit, good. If not, then you can cut it down.' "

Caring for
Others Is
Above
Keeping
the Law

Luke 13:10-17

Jesus was teaching in one of the synagogues on the Sabbath. There was a woman who had a spirit that had crippled her for eighteen years. She was bowed over and could not stand straight. When Jesus saw her, he called to her, and said, "Woman, you are freed from your infirmity." He laid his hands on her and immediately she stood up straight. And she glorified God.

The leader of the synagogue was indignant, because Jesus had healed the woman on the Sabbath. He said to the people, "There are six days when men can work. Come on those days and be healed, but not on the Sabbath day."

The Lord answered, "You hypocrite, wouldn't any of you untie his ox or his donkey from the stall on the Sabbath and lead him to water? This woman is a daughter of Abraham. Satan has crippled her for eighteen years. Shouldn't she be freed from this affliction on the Sabbath?"

When he said these things, all his opponents were ashamed. And all the people rejoiced for the glorious things that he did.

Then he said, "What is the kingdom of God like? What should I compare it to? It is like a mustard seed, which a man planted in his garden. It grew and became a great tree and the birds of the air nested in its branches."

Then he said, "What is the kingdom of God like? It is like leaven that a woman mixed into three measures of meal until it was all leavened."

Describing the Entrance to the Kingdom

The Great Tree and the Leavened Bread

Luke 13:18-30

Jesus went through the cities and villages, teaching, and journeying toward Jerusalem. Then someone said to him, "Lord, will only a few be saved?"

He said to them, "Strive to enter in at the narrow gate. Many will try to enter in and will not succeed. When the master of the house has stood up, and has shut the door, and you stand outside, and knock at the door saying, 'Lord, Lord, open to us,' he will say, 'I don't know you.' Then you

"There are last which will be first. . ."

Luke 13:22-35

will say, 'We have eaten and drunk in your presence, and you have taught in our streets.' But he will say, 'I tell you, I don't know you. Get away from me, you evil workers.' There will be weeping and gnashing of teeth when you will see Abraham, Isaac, Jacob, and all the prophets in the kingdom of God, and you yourselves cast out.

"And they will come from the east, and from the west, and from the north, and from the south, and will sit down in the kingdom of God. Listen, there are some who are last who will be first, and there are some who are first who will be last."

That same day, some Pharisees came to him, saying, "Get out. Leave here. Herod will kill you." He said to them, "You go and tell that fox, 'Look, I cast out devils and heal today and tomorrow; on the third day I will be perfected.' Nevertheless, I will live today, and tomorrow, and the day following. It is impossible for a prophet to die outside of Jerusalem.

"O Jerusalem, Jerusalem, you kill the prophets, and stone those who are sent to you. So often I would have gathered your children together like a hen gathers her brood under her wings, and you would not allow it! Look! Your temple is abandoned, emptied of God. I tell you the truth, you will not see me until the time comes when you say, 'Blessed is he that comes in the name of the Lord.' "

And it so happened on the Sabbath, as he went into the house of one of the chief Pharisees to eat a meal, they watched him carefully. There was a man in front of him whose body was sick and swollen. Jesus spoke to the lawyers and Pharisees, saying, "Is it lawful to heal on the Sabbath?" They said nothing. Jesus took the sick man, healed him, and let him go. Then he said, "Which of you who has a donkey or an ox fall into a pit, will not pull him out on the Sabbath?"

And he gave some advice to those who were invited to the meal, because he noticed how they chose the places of honor to recline at the table. "When you are invited to a wedding, do not sit in the place of honor. Why? A more honorable man than you may be invited. The host

"Whoever exalts himself will be abased. . ."

Luke 14:1-14

would then say to you, 'Give this man your place' and with shame you will sit in the lowest place. But when you are invited, go and sit down in the lowest place so that when the host comes he may say to you, 'Friend, go up higher.' Then you will be honored in the presence of those who sit eating with you.

"Whoever exalts himself will be abased; and he that humbles himself will be exalted."

Then he said to his host, "When you make a dinner, do not call your friends, your brothers, your relatives, or your rich neighbors. They can invite you in return, and so repay you. But when you make a feast, call the poor, the maimed, the lame, the blind, and you will be blessed. For they cannot repay you. You will be repaid at the resurrection of the righteous."

Invitations to the Kingdom

Luke 14:15-24

When one who sat eating with him heard these things, he said, "Blessed is he that will eat in the kingdom of God."

Then Jesus said, "A man made a great supper, and invited many. He sent his servant at supper time to tell those who were invited, 'Come, all things are ready.'

"And they all were the same, because they made excuses. The first said, 'I have bought a piece of land and I must go see it. Please have me excused.' And another said, 'I have bought five yoke of oxen. I must go and try them out. Please have me excused.' And another said, 'I have just been married, therefore I cannot come.'

"So the servant told his master these things. The master was angry, and said to his servant, 'Go out quickly into the streets and lanes of the town, and bring the poor, the maimed, the crippled, and the blind here to my feast.' The servant said, 'Master, we have done as you have commanded, and yet there is more room.' The master said to the servant, 'Go out into the roads and highways and compel people to come in, so that my house may be filled. I declare that none of those who were invited will taste of my dinner.' "

Great crowds were traveling with him. He turned and said to them, "Whoever comes to me and does not hate his father,

Count the Cost

Luke 14:25-35

mother, wife, children, brothers, and sisters —yes, even his own life—cannot be my disciple. Whoever does not bear his cross and follow me, cannot be my disciple.

"Which of you, intending to build a tower, does not sit down first and count the cost to learn whether he has sufficient money to finish it? Otherwise, after he has laid the foundation and is not able to finish it, everyone who sees it will mock him, saying, 'This man began to build, and was not able to finish.'

"Or what king who goes to war against another king, does not sit down first, and consider whether he is able, with ten thousand soldiers, to meet an army of twenty thousand? If he cannot, while the other army is still far away, he sends an ambassador, seeking peace.

"In the same way, you cannot be my disciple unless you forsake all that you have. Salt is good, but if the salt has lost its flavor, how can you make it salty again? It is not fit for the soil, or for the compost heap. You simply cast it out. If you are listening, try to understand."

Then all the publicans and sinners gathered around to hear him. And the Pharisees and scribes murmured, "This man welcomes sinners, and eats with them!"

Jesus spoke this parable to them: "If one of you had a hundred sheep and lost one of them, wouldn't you leave the ninety-nine sheep in the wilderness, and go after the lost sheep until you found it? And when you found it, wouldn't you pick it up, lay it on your shoulders, and rejoice? And when you got home you would call together your friends and neighbors, saying to them, 'Rejoice with me; for I have found my lost sheep.' I tell you, the same kind of joy will be in heaven over one sinner that repents, more than over ninety-nine righteous persons who need not repent."

If a woman has ten pieces of silver and loses one, doesn't she light a candle, sweep the house, and seek diligently until she finds it? When she has found it, she calls her friends and her neighbors together, saying, 'Rejoice with me; for I have found the piece of silver which I had lost.'

The Lost Sheep: the Work of the Son

Luke 15:1-7

The Lost Coin: the Work of the Spirit

Luke 15:8-10

Likewise, I tell you, there is joy in the presence of the angels of God over one sinner that repents."

The
Lost Son:
the Work
of the Father

Luke 15:11-32

And he said, "A man had two sons. The younger of them said to his father, 'Give me my inheritance.' And he divided the inheritance between his sons. Not many days after this, the younger son gathered all he had together, and journeyed into a faraway country. There he wasted all he had in wild living. When he had spent everything, a famine came to that land and he was in poverty. So he went to work for a citizen of the country who sent him into his fields to feed swine. He had to eat husks that the swine ate. No one gave anything to him.

"Then he started to think about his situation. He said, 'How many of my father's hired servants have bread to spare? Yet I perish with hunger! I will go to my father, and say to him, "Father, I have sinned against heaven, and against you, and am no longer worthy to be called your son. Make me one of your hired servants."'

"He got up, and went to his father. But

his father saw him when he was still a great way off. He had compassion, and ran, and fell on his son's neck, and kissed him. The son said to him, "Father, I have sinned against heaven, and in your sight, and am no longer worthy to be called your son." '

"But the father said to his servants, 'Bring out the best robe, and put it on him; and put a ring on his hand, and shoes on his feet: And bring the fatted calf, kill it, and let's eat and be merry: Because my son was dead and is alive again; he was lost, and is found.' And they began to celebrate.

"The father's elder son was in the field. As he came near the house, he heard music and dancing, and called one of the servants to ask what was happening. The servant said to him, 'Your brother is come; and your father has killed the fatted calf, because he has welcomed him back safe and sound.'

"The older son was angry, and would not go in. So his father came out and begged him to come into the celebration. He answered his father, 'Look, I have served you all these years. I did everything you ever asked. Yet you never gave me a fatted calf so that I could throw a party with my friends. But as soon as your youngest son came home, the one who used up his inheritance with harlots, you have killed the fatted calf!'

"His father said, 'Son, you are always with me, and all that I have is yours. It was right that we should make merry, be glad, and celebrate. Your brother was dead, and is alive again! He was lost, and is found.' "

Four Warnings about Duty

Serve God or Mammon

Luke 16:1-18

Jesus said to his disciples, "There was a rich man who had a steward who was accused of wasting his goods. He called the steward, and said to him, 'What is this I hear about you? Give an account of your stewardship, for you may not be my steward much longer.'

"Then the steward said to himself, 'What will I do if my master takes my job from me? I cannot dig, and I am ashamed to beg. Aha! I know what I'll do, so that when I lose my job, these people will receive me into their houses.'

"So he called on every one of his master's debtors. He said to the first, 'How much do you owe my master?' And he said, 'A hundred measures of oil.' The steward said, 'Take your bill, and sit down quickly, and write a check for fifty.' Then he said to another, 'How much do you owe?' And he said, 'A hundred measures of wheat.' The steward said to him, 'Take your bill, and write a check for eighty.'

"The master complimented the dishonest steward because he had done wisely. The children of this world are wiser than the children of light. So I say, make friends of unrighteous mammon so that, when you fail, they will receive you into eternal homes.

"He who is faithful in the least is also faithful in much. He that is dishonest in the least is also dishonest in much. If you have not been faithful in unrighteous mammon, who will commit to your trust the true riches? And if you have not been faithful in that which belongs to another man, who will give you that which is your own?

"No servant can serve two masters: for either he will hate the one, and love the other; or else he will hold to the one, and despise the other. You cannot serve God and mammon."

The Pharisees (who were greedy) heard these things, and ridiculed Jesus. He said to them, "You excuse your behavior to everyone, but God knows your hearts. That which is highly respectable among men is an abomination in the sight of God.

"The law and the prophets were in effect until John came. Since that time, the kingdom of God has been announced, and everyone tries to enter it by force. But it is easier for heaven and earth to pass away than one stroke of the letter of the law to fail. Whoever divorces his wife and marries another, commits adultery. Whoever marries her that is put away from her husband commits adultery.

Hear
the Word
of God

Luke 16:19-31

There was a rich man, who was clothed in purple and fine linen, and ate elegantly every day. There was a beggar named Lazarus, who lay at his gate, full of sores, waiting to be fed with the crumbs that fell from the rich man's table. The dogs came and licked his sores.

"It so happened that the beggar died and was carried by the angels to be comforted by Abraham. The rich man also died, and was buried. In hell, he looked up in torment, and saw Abraham far off with Lazarus in his arms. He cried and said, 'Father Abraham, have mercy on me, and send Lazarus, that he may dip the tip of his finger in water, and cool my tongue; for I am suffering in this flame.'

"But Abraham said, 'Son, remember that in your lifetime you had all your good things, and likewise Lazarus had the evil things. But now he is comforted and you are suffering. Not only this, between us and you there is a great chasm. Anyone who would try to pass from here to there cannot. Nor can anyone pass from you to us.'

"Then the rich man said, 'I pray, father, that you would send Lazarus to my father's house, to my five brothers, so that he may tell them about me. Otherwise, they will also come into this place of suffering.' Abraham said to him, 'They have Moses and the prophets. Let them hear them.' And he said, 'No, father Abraham. If someone went to them from the dead, they would repent.' And Abraham said to him, 'If they do not listen to Moses and the prophets, then they will not be persuaded by someone who rises from the dead.' "

Forgive Others

Luke 17:1-6

Then he said to the disciples, "It is inevitable that causes for stumbling will come; but woe to him through whom they come! It is better for him that a millstone be hung about his neck, and he be cast into the sea, than that he should offend one of these little ones.

"Be careful: If your brother sins against you, rebuke him. If he repents, forgive him. If he sins against you seven times in one day, and seven times a day turns to you, saying, 'I repent,' you must forgive him."

The apostles said to the Lord, "Increase our faith." The Lord said, "If your faith were only as big as a mustard seed, you could say to this mulberry tree, 'Be uprooted and be planted in the sea,' and it would obey you.

Which one of you, with a servant plowing or feeding cattle, would say to him when he is come in from work, 'Go, sit down and eat'? Wouldn't you actually say to him, 'Prepare my meal, and serve it to me. When I have eaten and drunk then you can eat and drink'?

"Would you thank your servant because he did the things that were expected of him? I don't think so. The same is true for you. When you have done all the things which are expected of you, here is what you will say, 'I am an unprofitable servant. I have only done my duty.'"

Revealing
the
Resurrection
in Bethany

Lazarus Sleeps

John 11:1-16

A man named Lazarus was sick. He lived in Bethany, the town of Mary and her sister Martha. (This is the same Mary who anointed the Lord with ointment and wiped his feet with her hair. Lazarus was her brother.) Therefore, his sisters sent word to Jesus, saying, "Lord, Lazarus, whom you love, is sick."

When Jesus heard this, he said, "This sickness will not lead to death, rather it is for the glory of God, so that the Son of God can be glorified through it."

Jesus loved Martha, her sister, and Lazarus. When he heard that Lazarus was sick, he waited two days in the place where he was.

After that he said to his disciples, "Let's go into Judea again." His disciples said to him, "Master, lately the Jews have wanted to stone you. Are you going there again?" Jesus answered, "Aren't there twelve hours in the day? If a man walks in the day, he won't stumble, because he sees the light of this world. But if a man walks in the night, he stumbles because there is no light in him."

After he said these things to them, he said, "Our friend Lazarus is asleep. But I go to awaken him out of sleep." Then his disciples said, "Lord, if he is asleep, he'll be fine." However, Jesus was speaking of his death, though they thought that he was simply talking about sleeping.

Then Jesus said to them plainly: "Lazarus is dead. And I am glad for your sakes that I was not there. Why? So that you may believe. Let's go to him." Then Thomas (the one called the Twin) said to his fellow disciples, "Let's go also so that we may die with him."

When Jesus came to Bethany, he found that Lazarus had been in the grave for four days. Bethany was near Jerusalem, about two miles away. Many Jews from Jerusalem came to Martha and Mary to comfort them because their brother had died. As soon as Martha heard that Jesus was coming, she went out to meet him; but Mary stayed in the house. Martha said to Jesus, "Lord, if you had been here, my brother would not have died. But I know that, even now, whatever you ask of God, God will give it to you."

Jesus said to her, "Your brother will rise again." Martha said, "I know that he will rise again in the resurrection on the last day." Jesus said to her, "I am the resurrection, and the life. Those who believe in me, even though they die, will live. Whoever lives and believes in me will never die. Do you believe this?" She said to him, "Yes, Lord! I believe that you are the Christ, the Son of God, which should come into the world."

When she said this, she went to Mary

Jesus
Weeps

John 11:17-37

her sister and whispered, "The Master has come and is calling for you." As soon as Mary heard this, she quickly arose and came to him. Jesus had not yet come into the town, but was still in the place where Martha met him.

The Jews who were comforting her in the house saw Mary rise up quickly and go out. They followed her, saying to each other, "She is going to the grave to weep." When Mary came to where Jesus was, she saw him, fell down at his feet, and said, "Lord, if you had been here, my brother would not have died."

When Jesus saw her weeping (the Jews who came with her were also weeping), Jesus groaned within and was troubled. He said, "Where is his tomb?" They said, "Lord, come and see."

Then Jesus wept. The Jews said, "Look how he loved him!" Some of them said, "Couldn't this man, who opens the eyes of the blind, have prevented this man from dying?"

Jesus
Groans

John 11:38-44

Jesus again groaned within. Then he came to the grave, which was a cave. A large stone lay upon it. Jesus said, "Take away the stone." Martha, Lazarus's sister, said, "Lord, by this time he stinks, he has been dead four days." Jesus said to her, "Didn't I say to you that if you would believe, you would see the glory of God?"

Then they took away the stone from the mouth of the cave. Jesus lifted up his eyes and said, "Father, I thank you that you have heard me. I know that you always hear me. I have said this for the sake of the people who stand by—that they may believe that you have sent me." When he had said this, he cried out with a loud voice, "Lazarus, come forth!"

The dead man came out with his hands and feet wrapped in strips of cloth and his face covered with a cloth. Jesus said to them, "Untie him and let him go."

Then many of the Jews who came to comfort Mary, and had seen the things that Jesus did, believed in him. But some of them went away to the Pharisees and told them what Jesus had done.

Then the chief priests and the Pharisees gathered in a council and asked

The Conspiracy Begins

John 11:45-53

each other, "What shall we do? This man does so many miracles. If we let him alone, everyone will believe in him. Then the Romans will come and destroy our holy place and take away our right to be a nation." One of them, named Caiaphas, who was the high priest that year, said to them, "You are all ignorant. It is best for us that one man would die for the people than for all the people to perish." But when he said this, Caiaphas was not speaking on his own. He was high priest that year, so this was a prophecy that Jesus would die for the nation of Israel. And not only for the Jewish nation, but also to gather together as one all the scattered children of God. So from that day on they made plans to put Jesus to death.

Retreating
from Danger
Again
to Ephraim

John 11:54-57

This is why Jesus no longer lived openly among the Jews. Instead he went to Ephraim, an area near the wilderness. He remained there with his disciples.

The time for the Jewish Passover was near. Before it came, many people went from the countryside to Jerusalem to purify themselves. They looked for Jesus. As they stood in the temple, they spoke among themselves. "What do you think? Will he come to the feast, or not?" The chief priests and the Pharisees had commanded that anyone who knew where Jesus was should tell them so that they could arrest him.

Describing the Time of His Second Coming

A Stranger Gives Thanks *between Galilee and Samaria*

Luke 17:11-19

And it happened that as he went to Jerusalem, he passed through Samaria and Galilee. As he entered into a certain village, ten men that were lepers met him. They stood far off, lifted up their voices, and cried, "Jesus, Master, have mercy on us." When he saw them, Jesus said to them, "Go show yourselves to the priests." And as they went on their way, they were cleansed.

One of them saw that he was healed, and turned back. With a loud voice, he glorified God, fell down on his face at Jesus' feet, and gave him thanks. This man was a Samaritan. Jesus said, "Weren't ten men cleansed? Where are the other nine? Only this stranger returned to give glory to God." Jesus said to him, "Get up and go on your way, your faith has made you whole."

"As it was in the days of Noah..."

Luke 17:20-27

When the Pharisees demanded that he tell them when the kingdom of God would come, he answered, "The kingdom of God is not coming in things which can be seen. People will not say, 'Look it is here!' Or, 'Look it is there!' Why? Because the kingdom of God is here among you."

He said to the disciples, "The time will come when you will desire to see one of the days of the Son of Man, and you will not see it. They will say to you, 'Look here,' or 'Look there.' Do not go or follow them. For just like the lightning that flashes out of one part of the sky lights up the whole sky, so will the Son of Man be when he comes.

"But first he must suffer many things and be rejected by this generation.

"As it was in the days of Noah, so will it be in the days of the Son of Man. They ate, they drank, they married wives, they were given in marriage, until the day that Noah entered the ark, and the flood came and destroyed them all.

"Remember Lot's wife"

Luke 17:28-37

It will also be like the days of Lot. They ate, they drank, they bought, they sold, they planted, they built; but the same day that Lot went out of Sodom, it rained fire and brimstone from heaven, and destroyed them all.

"This is how it will be in the day when the Son of Man is revealed on earth. On that day, if you are on the housetop, and your stuff is in the house, do not come down to take it away. If you are in the field, likewise do not return back home. Remember Lot's wife. Whoever will seek to save his life will lose it; and whoever will lose his life will preserve it.

"Listen. In that night there will be two men in one bed. One will be taken and the other will be left behind. Two women will be grinding flour together. One will be taken and the other left behind. Two men will be in the field. One will be taken and the other left behind." They said to him, "Where, Lord?" And he said, "Wherever the corpse is, there the vultures will be gathered together."

Jesus spoke a parable in order to teach them that people should always pray, and not grow weary: "There was a judge in a

Three Ways to Pray for Christ's Second Coming

certain town who did not fear God or respect other people. And there was a widow in that town who came to him, saying, 'Give me justice against my opponent.' But he would not do this, at least for a while. But eventually he said to himself, 'Though I do not fear God, or respect people, I will give this widow justice because she troubles me so much. Otherwise, she will wear me out with all her requests.' "

And then the Lord said, "Listen to what that unrighteous judge said. Don't you think that God will give justice to his own elected people—those who cry day and night to him? Will he delay in helping them? I tell you that he will quickly give them justice. Yet, when the Son of Man comes, will he find faith on the earth?"

And he spoke the following parable to those who trusted that they were righteous in themselves, and at the same time, despised others: "Two men went up into the temple to pray; one was a Pharisee, and the other was a tax collector. The Pharisee stood up alone and prayed like this: 'God, I thank you, that I am not like other people, shabby thieves and adulterers, or even like that tax collector over there. I fast twice a week and I give ten percent of all my income.'

"And the tax collector, standing far off, would not even lift up his eyes to heaven, but he beat upon his breast, saying, 'God be merciful to me, I am a sinner.' I tell you, this man went back to his house with God's approval, but the other did not. Every one who exalts himself will be abased. He that humbles himself will be exalted."

When Jesus finished saying these things, he departed from Galilee, and came to the border of Judea beyond the Jordan River. Large crowds followed him and he healed them there. And the Pharisees came and tempted him, saying, "Does the law allow for a man to divorce his wife for any reason?"

He answered, "Haven't you read that the one who made them at the beginning 'made them male and female,' and said, 'For this cause will a man leave his father and mother, and will be joined to his wife

The Work West of the Jordan River

Concerning Marriage and Divorce

Matt. 19:1-12
Mark 10:1-12

and the two will be one flesh'? Therefore they are no longer two, but one flesh. So, what God has joined together, let no one separate."

They said to him, "Why then did Moses tell us we can dismiss a wife after we give her a divorce document?" He answered, "Moses allowed you to divorce your wives because of the hardness of your hearts. But in the beginning it was not like this. I say to you, whoever divorces his wife, except for the reason of fornication, and marries another woman, commits adultery. And whoever marries a divorced woman also commits adultery."

His disciples asked him, "If this is the case, it is not good to marry." But he said, "Not everyone can understand this, only those to whom it is given. Some eunuchs were that way from the time they were born. Other eunuchs were made eunuchs by others. And some eunuchs have made themselves eunuchs for the sake of the kingdom of heaven. Accept this if you can."

Then little children were brought to him so that he could put his hands on them and pray. But the disciples rebuked the people who brought them.

Concerning Children
Matt. 19:13-15
Mark 10:13-16
Luke 18:15-17

But when Jesus saw this he was very displeased and said to them, "Allow the little children to come to me. Don't stop them. For the kingdom of heaven belongs to people who are like these children. I tell you, whoever does not receive the kingdom of God as a little child will not enter in there."

He took the children up in his arms, laid his hands on them and blessed them. Then he departed.

Then someone came and said to him, "Good Master, what good thing should I do so that I may have eternal life?" And Jesus said to him, "Why do you call me 'good'? Only one is good; that is, God. If you want to enter into eternal life, keep the commandments." He said to Jesus, "Which commandment should I keep?"

On Inheriting Eternal Life

Matt. 19:16-30
Mark 10:17-31
Luke 18:18-30

Jesus said, "Do not murder, do not commit adultery, do not steal, do not bear false witness, honor your father and your mother, and love your neighbor as yourself." The young man said to him, "I have kept all these laws since I was a boy. What else should I do?"

Jesus said to him, "If you want to be perfect, go and sell everything you have, give the money to the poor, and come and follow me. Then you will have treasure in heaven." But when the young man heard this, he went away sorrowful, because he had many possessions.

Then Jesus said to his disciples, "I say to you, it will be hard for a rich man to enter into the kingdom of heaven. It is easier for a camel to go through the eye of a needle, than for a rich man to enter into the kingdom of God." When his disciples heard this, they were amazed, "Who then can be saved?" they asked. Jesus looked at them and said, "With people this is impossible, but with God all things are possible."

Peter said to him, "Look at us, we have forsaken everything and followed you. What will our reward be?" Jesus said, "In the restoration, when the Son of Man sits on his glorious throne, you who have followed me will sit upon twelve thrones, judging the twelve tribes of Israel. Every one that has left behind houses, or brothers, or sisters, or father, or mother, or wife, or children, or lands, for my name's sake, will receive a hundred times what he left behind, and will inherit everlasting life. But many that are first will be last, and the last will be first.

The kingdom of heaven can be compared to a landowner who went out early in the morning to hire laborers for his vineyard. When he had agreed to pay the laborers a fair wage, he sent them into his vineyard. He went out at about nine in the morning and saw others standing idle in the marketplace. He said to them, 'You go to work in the vineyard also and I will pay you a fair wage.' And they went to work.

"He went out again about noon, and again at three, and did the same thing. Then, at about five that afternoon, he went out and found others standing around doing nothing. He said to them, 'Why are you standing here all day doing nothing?' They said to him, 'Because no one has hired us.' He answered, 'You go

More About Inheriting Eternal Life

Matt. 20:1-16

also and work in my vineyard. You will receive a fair wage.'

"When evening came, the owner of the vineyard said to his manager, 'Call the laborers and give them their pay; begin from the last ones I hired and finally pay the first ones.' The workers who were hired at about five in the afternoon received a day's pay. So when the ones who were hired first came, they thought that they would receive more than this. But they too received a day's pay.

"When they had received their pay, they complained to the landowner, 'The ones you hired last only worked one hour, and you have paid them the same as us, even though we worked hard through the heat of the day.' He answered one of them, 'Friends, I didn't wrong you. Didn't you agree with me for a fair wage? Take what is yours and go on your way. I will give to the last ones the same pay as I have given to you. Am I not allowed to do what I want with my own money? Are you evil because I am good?' So the last will be first, and the first last: for many are called, but few chosen."

They were all on the road going up to Jerusalem. Jesus was walking ahead of them. As they followed him along the road, they were amazed at him, and afraid. He took the twelve aside and told them about the things that would happen to him. He said "Look, we are going up to Jerusalem. There the Son of Man will be handed over to the chief priests and the scribes. They will condemn him to death and will deliver him to the Gentiles, who will mock him, whip him, spit upon him, and kill him. On the third day, he will rise again."

Then the mother of Zebedee's children came to him with her sons. She worshipped him, and asked him for a favor. He said to her, "What do you want?" She told him, "Grant that my two sons may sit at your right hand and your left, in your kingdom."

But Jesus said, "You do not know what you are asking. Can you drink the cup that I will drink? Or be baptized with the baptism that I am about to be baptized with?" They said to him, "Yes, we can." Jesus said to them, "Yes, you will drink of the cup that I drink of and experience the baptism that I am about to be baptized with. But I cannot promise that you will sit at my right and at my left. This honor will be given to those for whom my Father prepares it."

When the other ten disciples heard about this, they were displeased with James and John. So Jesus called them all to him and said, "You know that the rulers of the Gentiles lord it over them, and their great ones oppress them. But it will not be like this among you. Whoever will be great among you, will be your servant. And whoever is the first among you, will serve everyone. For the Son of Man did not come to be served, but to serve and to give his life as a ransom for many."

Seeking and
Saving the
Lost

• The
Blind Man
at Jericho

Matt. 20:29-34
Mark 10:46-52
Luke 18:25-43

As he came near Jericho, a blind man sat begging by the roadside. He heard the crowd pass by and asked, "What is happening?" They told him that Jesus of Nazareth was passing by. And so he cried out, saying, "Jesus! Son of David! Have mercy on me." The crowd rebuked him and told him to be quiet. But he cried out even more, "Son of David! Have mercy on me."

Jesus stopped and asked that the blind man be brought to him. When he was near, Jesus asked him, "What do you want me to do for you?" The man said, "Lord, I want to receive my sight." Jesus said, "Receive your sight then. Your faith has saved you." Immediately he could see, and followed Jesus, glorifying God. When all the people saw it, they praised God.

Jesus entered Jericho and passed through the town. And there was a man named Zaccheus, who was the chief tax collector, and so was rich. He wanted to see who Jesus was, but he couldn't, because the crowd was too thick and he was a short man. So he ran ahead and climbed up into a sycamore tree to see Jesus, because he was going to pass that way. When Jesus came to that place, he looked up, saw Zaccheus, and said to him, "Zaccheus, hurry up and come down here, because today I must stay at your house."

And he quickly came down and happily received him into his house. Everyone who saw this grumbled, "He has gone to

• The
Short Man

Luke 19:1-10

be the guest of a man who is a sinner." Zaccheus stood there and said to Jesus, "Lord, I will give half of my property to the poor. If I have taken any thing from any man falsely, I will repay him four times that much." Jesus said to him, "Today salvation has come to this house, because Zaccheus is a child of Abraham. For the Son of Man is come to seek and to save that which was lost."

The Parable of the Audits

Luke 19:11-27

As they listened, he told them a parable. He did this because they were near Jerusalem, and because they thought that the kingdom of God would appear immediately. He said, "A nobleman went into a far away country to receive the authority of his kingdom, and then return. He called his ten servants, and gave them each the same amount of money, and said to them, 'Do business with this until I return.' But the citizens of his country hated him, and so they sent a message after him, saying, 'We do not want this man to rule us.'

"When he returned with the power of his kingdom, he called these ten servants (the ones to whom he had given the money). He wanted to know how much each one had earned with his money.

"The first one came saying, 'Lord, I made ten times the amount you gave me.' He said to the servant, 'Well done, good servant. You have been faithful in a little, so you can have authority over ten cities in my kingdom.'

"And the second servant came, saying, 'Lord, I gained five times the amount you gave me.' He said, 'You can rule over five cities.'

"Another came, saying, 'Lord, look, here is your money. I kept it wrapped in a cloth. I was afraid of you. You are an austere man. You take away what you do not deposit, and you harvest what you do not sow.' He said to this servant, 'I will judge you with your own words, you wicked servant. You know that I am an austere man, collecting what I don't deposit, and harvesting what I don't sow. Why then didn't you at least deposit my money in the bank, so that I might have collected my money with interest?' He said to those who stood nearby, 'Take the money from him and give it to the one who earned ten times the amount.

"'I tell you, to those who have, more will be given; and to those that have not, that which he has will be taken away from him. As for my enemies, who would not have me rule over them, bring them here, and kill them in front of me.' "

Love, Greed, and Jealousy
in Bethany

Matt. 26:6-13
Mark 14:3-9
John 12:1-11

Then, six days before the Passover, Jesus came to Bethany, to the house of Simon the leper where Lazarus lived (the man who had died, whom Jesus had raised from the dead). There they made him a supper. Martha served and Lazarus was among those who sat at the table with him.

Then Mary took an alabaster jar containing a pound of very costly ointment made of spikenard. She broke the seal of the jar and poured the ointment on Jesus' head, anointed his feet, and wiped his feet with her hair. The house was filled with the odor of the ointment.

Then one of his disciples said (this was Judas Iscariot, Simon's son, the one who would betray him), "This ointment could have been sold for a small fortune, and the money given to the poor!" He said this not because he cared for the poor, but because he was a thief. He was in charge of the disciples' money, and occasionally stole some of it for himself.

Then Jesus said, "Let her alone, she has done all she could in preparation for the day I am buried. You always have the poor with you. But you won't always have me here. But listen, wherever this gospel is preached in all the world, there the story of what this woman has done will be told in her memory."

Many Jews knew that he was there and so they came to Bethany. But they did not come just to see Jesus. They also wanted to see Lazarus, whom he had raised from the dead. Yet the chief priests considered how they could put Lazarus to death. Why? Because of him many Jews left them and believed in Jesus.

Chapter Seven

The Week of Christ's Death

When they came near Jerusalem, to Bethphage on the Mount of Olives, Jesus sent two disciples ahead and told them, "Go into the nearby village, and you will find a donkey on which no one has ever ridden. She will be tied there with her colt. Untie them both, and bring them to me. If anyone says anything to you about this, answer, 'The Lord needs them.' Right away he will send them with you." All this was done, so that the words of the prophet would be fulfilled: "Tell the daughter of Zion, fear not, daughter of Zion. Look,

Sunday

The King Rides a Donkey

Matt. 21:1-11
Mark 11:1-11
Luke 19:28-44
John 12:12-19

your King comes to you, meekly sitting upon a donkey, and a colt, the foal of a donkey."

The disciples went and did as Jesus said. They found the colt tied by a door at the intersection of two streets, and untied her. The people that stood there said, "What are you doing, untying the colt?" They said to them what Jesus told them. And they let them go on their way.

They brought the donkey and the colt, and put some of their clothes over their backs, and Jesus sat on them. And a large crowd spread their garments in the road. Others cut down branches from the trees and laid them in the road. Crowds went ahead of him, and those who followed him cried, "Hosanna to the Son of David! Blessed is he that comes in the name of the Lord! Hosanna in the highest! Blessed is the King of Israel that comes in the name of the Lord."

His disciples did not understand these things at first. But when Jesus was glorified, they remembered that these things were written about him, and that they had done these things for him. The people who were with him when he called Lazarus out of his grave, and raised him from the dead, told many others about it. This is why the people came out to meet him: They heard that he had done this miracle. The Pharisees said among themselves, "Look, we've lost. The whole world has gone after him."

When he came into Jerusalem, all the city was affected. They said, "Who is this?" And the crowd said, "This is Jesus, the prophet of Nazareth of Galilee." And Jesus entered into the temple. When he had looked around at everything, evening had come. So he went out to Bethany with the twelve.

In the morning, as he returned into the city, he was hungry. He saw a fig tree along the road, came to it, and found nothing on it, only leaves. He said to the fig tree, "No fruit will grow on you from now on." Soon the fig tree withered away.

Monday

The Fruitless Fig Tree

Matt. 21:18-19

There were some Greeks there that came up to worship at the feast. They came to Philip (who was from Bethsaida of

The Wheat Seed's Death

John 12:20-36

Galilee), and asked, "Sir, we want to see Jesus." Philip told Andrew. And so Andrew and Philip told Jesus.

Jesus answered the Greeks, "The time has come for the Son of Man to be glorified. I say to you, unless a wheat seed falls into the ground and dies, it exists alone. But if it dies, it brings forth many more grains of wheat. He that loves his life will lose it; and he that hates his life in this world will keep it for eternal life. If anyone serves me, let him follow me. My servant will be where I am. If anyone serves me, my Father will honor him.

"My soul is troubled. Should I pray, 'Father, save me from this hour?' But this is why I came this far. Father, glorify your name." Then a voice came from heaven, saying, "I have both glorified it, and will glorify it again." The people who stood nearby, and heard this, said that it thundered. Others said, "An angel spoke to him."

Jesus said, "This voice did not come because of me, but for your sake. Now the judgment of this world has come. Now will the prince of this world be cast out.

And if I am lifted up from the earth on a cross, I will draw all humanity to me." He said this to indicate what kind of death he would die.

The people answered, "We have learned from Scripture that Christ lives forever. How can you say, 'The Son of Man must be lifted up on a cross?' Who is this Son of Man?" Jesus said to them, "The light is with you for a little while longer. Walk while you have the light, or else darkness will come upon you. Whoever walks in darkness does not know where he is going.

"While you have light, believe in the light, that you may be the children of light." Jesus spoke these things, departed, and hid from them.

Even though he had done so many miracles for them, they still did not believe in him. This fulfilled the saying of Isaiah the prophet: "Lord, who has believed our report? To whom has the strength of the Lord been revealed?"

They could not believe, because, as Isaiah said, "He has blinded their eyes and

Declaring
the Focus
of Our Faith

John 12:37-50

hardened their heart, so that they should not see with their eyes, nor understand with their heart, and be changed, and I could heal them." Isaiah said these things when he saw God's glory, and spoke of him.

Still, many of the chief rulers believed in Jesus. But they did not admit it, for fear that the Pharisees would put them out of the synagogue. (The Pharisees loved the praise of men more than the praise of God.)

Then Jesus cried out, "He that believes in me, believes not in me, but in him that sent me. And he that sees me sees him that sent me. I am come as a light into the world, so that whoever believes in me would not live in darkness. If any one hears my words, and does not believe, I will not judge him. I did not come to judge the world, but to save the world.

"He that rejects me, and does not receive my words, has a judge. It is the words that I have spoken. These will judge him on the last day. For I have not spoken of myself, but the Father who sent me, he gave me a commandment, what I should say, and what I should speak. And I know that his commandment is life everlasting. Whatsoever I speak, therefore, even as the Father said to me, so I speak."

Jesus went into the temple of God and cast out all those who bought and sold offerings and sacrifices there. He overthrew the tables of the money changers, and the benches of those who sold doves. He would not allow any one to carry any vessels through the temple, and said to them, "It is written, 'My house will be called the house of prayer for all nations,' but you have made it a den of thieves." When the scribes and chief priests heard about this, they looked for a way to destroy Jesus, because they were afraid of him, and because all the people were astonished at his teaching.

The Godless Temple

Matt. 21:12-17
Mark 11:15-19
Luke 19:45-48

Blind and lame people came to him in the temple, and he healed them. The chief priests and scribes saw the wonderful things that he did and heard the children crying in the temple, saying, "Hosanna to the Son of David." They were quite displeased about this, and said to him, "Do you hear what these children say?" Jesus said, "Yes. Haven't you read, 'Out of the mouth of babes and sucklings I have perfected praise?' " Then he left them and went out of the city into Bethany to spend the night.

Tuesday

The Lesson of the Fig Tree

Matt. 21:20-22
Mark 11:20-25

In the morning, they passed by the fig tree and saw that it was dried up from the roots. Peter remembered and said to Jesus, "Master, look, the fig tree that you cursed is withered away." When the disciples saw it, they marveled, "How quickly the fig tree withered away!"

Jesus answered them, "Have faith in God. I tell you the truth, if you have faith, and doubt not, you will not only do this which is done to the fig tree, but also if you will say to this mountain, 'Be removed, and be cast into the sea,' and will not doubt, but will believe that those things will happen, you will have whatever you say.

"Therefore, I say, whatever you desire, when you pray, believe that you will receive it, and you will. When you stand and pray, if you have anything against anyone, forgive him. Then your Father in heaven will forgive you your own sins."

Jesus came into the temple. The chief priests and the elders of the people came to him as he was teaching, and said, "By whose authority do you do these things?" Jesus answered, "I will ask you one thing. John's baptism, was it of heaven, or of men? If you answer me, I will tell you by what authority I do these things."

They spoke among themselves: "If we say, 'From heaven'; he will say to us, 'Why didn't you believe him?' And we can't say, 'Of men,' because we are afraid of the people. They all think John is a prophet." So they answered Jesus, "We don't know." He said to them, "Neither will I tell you by whose authority I do these things.

"What do you think? A man had two sons. He came to the first and said, 'Son, go work today in my vineyard.' He answered, 'I will not.' But afterward he changed his mind and went. The man came to his second son, and said the same thing. The son answered, 'I will go, sir.' And he did not go.

"Which of the two did his father's

Warning the Religious Leaders

• The Parable of Two Sons and a Vineyard

Matt. 21:23-32
Mark 11:27-33
Luke 20:1-8

will?" They answered, "The first." Jesus said, "I tell you the truth, the publicans and the harlots will go into the kingdom of God before you. Why? Because John came to you in righteousness, and you did not believe him, but the publicans and the harlots did. When you saw him, you did not repent and believe him.

• The Parable of a Son Slain in a Vineyard

Matt. 21:33-46
Mark 12:1-12
Luke 20:9-19

Listen to another parable: There was a land owner who planted a vineyard, planted a hedge around it, dug a winepress in it, built a tower, rented it to farmers, and went away to a far country. When the time to harvest the fruit came, he sent servants to the farmers to get some of the harvest. The farmers took his servants, beat one, killed another, and stoned another.

"So he sent some other servants, more than the first time. The farmers did the same thing. Last of all he sent his son to them, thinking, 'They will respect my son.' But when the farmers saw his son, they said to each other, 'This is the heir; let's kill him, and seize his inheritance.' They caught him, cast him out of the vineyard, and killed him.

"When the lord of the vineyard comes back, what will he do to those farmers?" They answered, "He will miserably destroy those wicked men, and rent the vineyard to other farmers who will deliver the harvest to him in season."

Jesus said, "Have you ever read in the Scriptures, 'The stone which the builders rejected has become the head of the cornerstone of the building. This is the Lord's doing, and it is marvelous in our eyes'? This is why I say to you—the kingdom of God will be taken from you, and given to a nation that delivers the fruit of the kingdom to God. Whoever will fall on this stone will be broken. But whomever it falls upon it will grind to powder."

When the chief priests and Pharisees heard Jesus' parables, they understood that he was talking about them. They wanted to seize him, but they feared the crowds, because they thought he was a prophet.

Jesus spoke to them again in parables: "The kingdom of heaven is like a king who prepared a marriage for his son. He sent out his servants to call those who

• The Parable of the Called and the Chosen

Matt. 22:1-14

were invited to the wedding. But they would not come.

"So he sent out other servants, and told them, 'Tell those whom I have invited, Look, I have prepared my dinner: my oxen and my calves are killed, and all things are ready. Come to the marriage.' But they did not take it seriously and went their way. One went to his farm, and another to his store. Others took the servants, beat, and killed them. When the king heard of this, he was incensed, sent his army, destroyed the murderers, and burned their town.

"Then he said to his servants, 'The wedding is ready, but those who were invited were not worthy to attend. So go to the highways and invite to the marriage as many as you can find.' So the servants went out to the highways and gathered together as many people as they could find, both bad and good. And so the wedding was provided with guests.

"Then the king came in to see the guests. He saw a man who was not dressed for the occasion. He said to him, 'Friend, how did you get in here improperly dressed?' The man was speechless. The king told the servants, 'Tie him up, take him away, and cast him out into the darkness.' There will be weeping and gnashing of teeth, because many are called, but few are chosen."

So they watched Jesus and sent spies, who pretended to be good men and tried to catch him saying something wrong, and so deliver him to the power and authority of the governor.

And the Pharisees considered how they could entangle him in his words, and sent out their disciples with the Herodians, who asked, "Master, we know that you are true, and teach the way of God in truth. You are impartial and do not play favorites. So tell us: Do you think it is lawful to give tribute to Caesar, or not?"

But Jesus knew they were wicked, and said, "Why do you try to trick me, you hypocrites? Show me the money you use for tribute." They brought him a penny. He said to them, "Whose image and name is on this coin?" They answered, "Caesar's." Then he said to them, "Give to

The Conspiracy Continues

• The Pharisees and the Image of Caesar

Matt. 22:15-22
Mark 12:13-17
Luke 20:20-26

Caesar the things that belong to Caesar. Give to God the things that belong to God." When they heard these words, they marveled, left him, and went on their way.

• The Sadducees and the God of the Living

Matt. 22:23-33
Mark 12:18-27
Luke 20:27-40

The same day the Sadducees came to him. (The Sadducees say that there is no resurrection.) They asked him, "Master, Moses said if a man dies, and has no children, his brother will marry his wife, and raise children to inherit his brother's property. Now seven brothers were once with us. The first had married, but he died without children and left his wife to his brother: This happened to the second brother, the third, and so forth to the seventh. Last of all, the wo-man died. In the resurrection, whose wife among the seven will she be? They all had been her husband."

Jesus answered, "You are mistaken because you do not know the Scriptures, or the power of God. In the resurrection, people do not get married. They are like the angels of God in heaven. Concerning the resurrection of the dead: Haven't you read what God spoke to you? God said, 'I am the God of Abraham, and the God of

Isaac, and the God of Jacob.' God is not the God of the dead, but of the living." When the crowd heard this, they were astonished at his teaching.

When the Pharisees heard that Jesus had silenced the Sadducees, they gathered around him. One of them, a lawyer, tried to trick him with a question: "Master, which is the great commandment in the law?"

• The Lawyer and The Great Commandment

Matt. 22:34-40
Mark 12:28-34

Jesus said to him, "'You shall love the Lord your God with all your heart, and with all your soul, and with all your mind.' This is the first and great commandment. And the second is similar, 'You shall love your neighbor like you love yourself.' All the law and the writings of the prophets are based on these two commandments."

While the Pharisees were gathered around, Jesus asked them, "What do you think of Christ? Whose son is he?" They answered, "The Son of David."

• Stopping the Conspirators' Questions

Matt. 22:41-46
Mark 12:35-37
Luke 20:41-44

He said to them, "Why then did David call him 'Lord,' saying, 'The Lord said to my Lord, sit at my right side until

I make your enemies a footstool for you?' If David called him 'Lord,' how can he be David's son?" No one was able to answer him a word. From that day on, nobody asked him any more questions. But the common people gladly listened to him.

Condemning Religious Hypocrites

• "The greatest will be your servant"

Matt. 23:1-12
Mark 12:38-40
Luke 20:45-47

Then Jesus spoke to the crowd, and to his disciples: "The scribes and the Pharisees represent Moses. So do whatever they teach you. But do not imitate their way of life. They teach but they don't act on their teaching. They load on heavy burdens that are hard for people to carry; but they themselves do not even try to carry them. Everything they do is so that they can be seen by others. They wear big prayer boxes, and long fringe on their robes. They love the best places at the feasts, and the prominent seats in the synagogues. They love to be greeted in the markets, and for people to call them, 'Rabbi, Rabbi.'

"But don't you be called Rabbi. Only one is your Master: Christ. You are all brothers. Do not call any man your father. One is your Father, who is in heaven. Nor be called masters. One is your master: Christ. He that is greatest among you will be your servant. Whoever will exalt himself will be abased. Whoever is humble will be exalted.

Woe to you, scribes and Pharisees, hypocrites! You shut people out of the kingdom of heaven because you don't go in yourselves, nor allow others to go in. Woe to you, scribes and Pharisees, hypocrites! You cheat widows out of their property, and make long, phony prayers. Therefore you will receive great damnation.

"Woe to you, scribes and Pharisees, hypocrites! You travel all around land and sea to make one convert, and then you make him twice as much a child of hell as you are. Woe to you, you blind guides. You say, 'It means nothing if you swear by the temple. But whoever swears by the gold of the temple is bound to his oath'! You blind fools. Which is greater, the gold, or the temple that makes the gold holy?

"You say that it means nothing to swear by the altar. But whoever swears by the gift that is on the altar is bound to

• "God has left your temple"

Matt. 23:13-39

keep his oath. You blind fools! Which is greater, the gift, or the altar that makes the gift holy? When you swear by the altar, you swear by everything on it. When you swear by the temple you also swear by God who lives there. Whoever swears by heaven, swears by the throne of God, and by him who sits on that throne.

"Woe to you, scribes and Pharisees, hypocrites! You pay the tiniest tithes of mint and anise and cummin, yet you have omitted the more important matters of the law—things like judgment, mercy, and faith. Yes, you should tithe, but you ignore these important things. You blind guides. You try to strain out a gnat while you are swallowing a camel.

"Woe to you, scribes and Pharisees, hypocrites! You make the outside of the cup and the platter clean, but within they are full of bribery and greed. You blind Pharisee, first clean within the cup and platter. Then the outside of them will be clean also. Woe to you, scribes and Pharisees, hypocrites! You are like white-washed tombs, which appear outwardly beautiful, but are full of dead men's bones and uncleanness. You are the same—outwardly you appear righteous, but within you are full of hypocrisy and iniquity.

"Woe to you, scribes and Pharisees, hypocrites! You build the tombs of the prophets, and decorate the graves of the godly people. And you say, 'If we had lived in the times of our ancestors, we would not have murdered the prophets like they did.' Think about what you are saying: You are the descendants of those who killed the prophets. So go ahead, finish what they started!

"You serpents, you generation of vipers, how can you escape the judgment of hell? Look, I will send you prophets, and wise men, and scholars. You will kill some of them, crucify others, and some you will whip in your synagogues and persecute from town to town. Because of this, you will be held accountable for all the righteous blood shed on the earth. This includes the blood of righteous Abel to the blood of Zechariah son of Berekiah, whom you murdered in the temple near the altar. I tell you the truth, all these things will come upon your generation.

"O Jerusalem, Jerusalem, you kill the prophets, and stone those who are sent to you from God. Many times I have wanted to gather your children together, like a hen gathers her chickens under her wings. But you would not have it! Look, God has left your temple. It is empty. Listen to what I say to you: You will not see me again, until the day you say, 'Blessed is he that comes in the name of the Lord.'"

• The Lesson of the Widow's Gift

Mark 12:41-44
Luke 21:1-4

Jesus sat near the temple's treasury and watched the people deposit money into the treasury. Many who were rich cast in a lot. Then a poor widow came and threw in two pennies. He called his disciples, and said, "I tell you the truth, This poor widow has given more than everyone else. They all gave out of their abundant wealth. But she gave all that she had in her poverty."

Speaking About the Future

• The Disciples' Future

Matt. 24:1-14
Mark 13:1-13
Luke 21:5-24

Jesus left the temple and his disciples pointed out to him all the temple buildings. Jesus said to them, "Do you see these things? Here is the truth—not one stone in them will be left upon another. It will all be torn down."

As he sat on the slope of the Mount of Olives, the disciples asked him privately: "Tell us, when will this happen? Will there be a sign to foretell the end of the world? What will be the sign of your coming?" Jesus answered them: "Be careful that no one deceives you. Many will come in my name, saying, 'I am Christ,' and will deceive many people. Also you will hear of wars and rumors about wars. Do not be troubled by this. All these things must happen, but this is not the end. For nation will rise up against nation, and kingdom against kingdom. There will be famines, plagues, and earthquakes in various places. These things signal only the beginning of sorrowful times.

"Take care of yourselves, because they will deliver you to councils for questioning. You will be beaten in their places of worship. You will be brought to judgment before rulers and kings because you believe in me. But you will simply be evidence against them. Then they will torture you, and kill you. And the whole world will hate you because you believe in me. At that time, many will fall away, betray one another, and hate one another. Many false prophets will appear and will deceive many. There will be such an overflow of evil that many people's love for God will grow cold.

"But when they lead you away, and bring you to judgment, don't worry about what you will say. Don't even consider it beforehand. Whatever is given you to say at the time, say that. Remember, it is not you who is speaking; it is the Holy Spirit. I will give you a voice and wisdom that your enemies will not be able to contradict or resist.

"The brother will betray his brother to death, and the father will betray his son. Children will rise up against their parents and cause them to be put to death. And you will be hated by everyone because you believe in me. But not a hair of your head will perish. So possess your souls in patience. Whoever endures to the end will be saved. And the gospel of the kingdom will be preached in all the world for a witness to the nations. Then the end will come.

When you see the abomination of desolation stand in the holy place (that which Daniel the prophet spoke about; let the reader pay attention), and when you see Jerusalem surrounded by armies, then you will know that the destruction of the city will come soon. Then the people in Judea should flee to the mountains. The man on the housetop should not come down to take anything out of his house. Neither should the man in the field return to get his clothes. Those in Jerusalem should depart, and the people in the country should not come into the city. Because these are the days of God's vengeance and all the things written in the Scriptures by the prophets will be fulfilled.

"But woe to the women who are pregnant, and those who are nursing their babies in those days! And pray that you don't have to flee in the winter, or on the Sabbath. Because there will be great distress in the land, and wrath upon the people. They will die by the edge of the sword and will be led away captive into many nations. And Jerusalem will be occupied by the Gentiles until the age of the

• Israel's Future

Matt. 24:15-22
Mark 13:14-20
Luke 21:20-24

Gentiles is complete.

"Then great tribulation will come such as has never been seen since the beginning of the world to this time. And unless those days are cut short, no one will be saved. But for the elect's sake, those days will be shortened.

• The Church's Future

Matt. 24:23-35
Mark 13:21-31
Luke 21:25-33

If any one says to you, 'Look, here is Christ,' or, 'There he is!' do not believe it. False Christs and false prophets will come who will perform great signs and wonders. So many in fact that, if it were possible, they will deceive the elect.

"So watch out. Remember, I have told you everything beforehand.

"If they say to you, 'Look! he is in the desert,' don't go. 'Look! he is in a secret place,' don't believe it. Do you know how lightning can flash in the east and light up the west? That's how it will be when the Son of Man comes. Where the dead body is, there the vultures gather.

"Immediately after the tribulation, the sun will be darkened, the moon will give no light, the stars will fall from heaven, and the powers of the heavens will be shaken. There will be signs in the sun, in the moon, and in the stars. On earth, the nations will be distressed and perplexed. The sea and the waves will roar. People's hearts will fail them for fear, looking for the things which are coming upon earth.

"And then the sign of the Son of Man will appear in heaven, all the tribes of the earth will mourn, and they will see the Son of Man coming in the clouds of heaven with power and great glory. He will send his angels with the loud sound of a trumpet to gather together his elect from the four winds—from one end of heaven to the other.

"Here is a parable about the fig tree: When its branches are still tender and put out leaves, you know that summer is near. Likewise, when you see all these things happen, know that the end is near, just outside the door. I tell you the truth, this generation will not pass away until all these things are fulfilled. Heaven and earth will pass away, but my words will not pass away.

The Final
Parables

• A
Warning
About
Watchfulness

Matt. 24:36-51
Mark 13:32-37
Luke 21:34-38

Be careful that your hearts are not taxed with overabundance, drunkenness, and cares of this life; so that the day will not come when you are unaware. It will come like a snare on everyone that lives on earth. So always watch and pray that you may escape all the things that will happen, that you may stand before the Son of Man.

"Be careful to watch and pray. You don't know when the time is. Because the Son of Man is like a man who takes a long journey, gives instructions to his servants, sets every man to work, and tells the porter to watch.

"So watch. You do not know when the master of the house will come back: in the evening, at midnight, or when the rooster crows at the break of dawn. If he comes suddenly, will he find you sleeping? So I say to everyone, watch.

"No one knows when that day will come; not even the angels of heaven. Only my Father knows. But, just like it was in the days of Noah, so will the days of the coming of the Son of Man be. Before the flood, they were eating and drinking, marrying and giving in marriage. Then Noah entered into the ark, but they knew nothing until the flood came and took them all away. This is what it will be like when the Son of Man comes.

"Two will be in the field; one will be taken, and the other left behind. Two women will be grinding at the mill; one will be taken, and the other left behind. So watch. You do not know when your Lord will come. But know this: If the man of the house had known when the thief was coming, he would have watched and not allowed his house to be invaded. So be ready. The Son of Man will come at an unexpected time.

"Who is a faithful and wise servant whom the master can trust to manage his household and feed his family every day? If the master returns and finds that his servant has done a good job; he will reward that servant. Listen to this: He will put him in charge of his entire estate. But if a servant is evil and says to himself, 'My master won't be back for a long time,' and begins to mistreat the other servants, and eat and drink with drunkards—his master will return unexpectedly, with no warning, and will cut him down, and throw him out among the hypocrites, where there is weeping and gnashing of teeth."

And so, in the daytime, Jesus taught in the temple. At night he went out of the city, and stayed on the slope of the Mount of Olives. All the people came early in the morning to see and hear him in the temple.

Wednesday

The Final Parables (continued)

• A Parable About Preparedness

Matt. 25:1-13

Then the kingdom of heaven will be like ten pure young women, who took lamps, and went out to meet a bridegroom. Five were wise, and five were foolish. The foolish took their lamps with no extra oil. The wise took jars of oil with their lamps. When the bridegroom was late in arriving, they all fell asleep.

"At midnight they heard the warning: 'Look! The bridegroom is coming, go out to meet him.' Then all the young women got up and prepared their lamps. But the foolish said to the wise, 'Give us some of your oil. Our lamps have gone out.' The wise answered, 'No, there might not be enough for us and for you. Go find someone selling oil and buy some for yourselves.'

"While they went to buy, the bridegroom came, and the young women who were ready went in with him to the marriage and the door was shut. Afterward, the other young women arrived, 'Lord, Lord, open to us,' they said. He answered, 'I really do not know you.' So watch; you do not know the day or the hour in which the Son of Man will come.

The kingdom of heaven is like this: A man was going to travel to a far country. He called his servants, and divided his wealth among them. To one he gave five parts, to another two parts, and to another one part. Each one was given the amount he was able to use. And the man left on his journey.

• The Parable of Profit

Matt. 25:14-30

"Then the servant who had the five parts traded with it, and doubled the amount. And the one who had two, did the same. But the servant who had received the one part dug a hole in the earth, and hid his master's money.

"After a long time, the servants' master came back and asked them how they had used his money. So the one that received five parts brought the five he had earned. 'Lord, you gave to me five parts of your wealth. Look, I have doubled that amount.' His master said, 'Well done! You are a good and faithful servant. You have been faithful over a few things, so I will make you ruler over many things. Let's celebrate!'

"The servant that received two parts brought the two he had earned. 'Lord, you gave me two parts of your wealth. Look, I have doubled that amount.' His master said, 'Well done! You are a good and faithful servant. You have been faithful over a few things, so I will make you ruler over many things. Let's celebrate!'

"Then the one who had received one part came and said, 'Lord, I know that you are a hard man who harvests what you have not planted, and gathers where you have not plowed. I was afraid, and hid your wealth in the ground. Look, here is what you gave me.' His master answered, 'You wicked, slothful servant! You knew that I harvest what I have not planted, and gather where I have not plowed. You ought to have at least put my money in the bank, then I could have received what I gave you with interest.

"'Take that portion of my wealth from him, and give it to the servant who made the five parts into ten. The ones who use what they are given, will have more in abundance. But those who do not will lose what they have. Throw this unprofitable servant outside into the darkness where there is weeping and gnashing of teeth.'

When the Son of Man comes with all the holy angels, he will sit upon the throne of his glory. All the people of the nations will gather in front of him and he will separate them like a shepherd divides his sheep from the goats. He will set the sheep to the right, and the goats on the left.

• The Separation of the Sheep from the Goats

Matt. 25:31-46

"Then the king will say to them on the right, 'Come, you are blessed by my Father, inherit the kingdom which has been prepared for you from the beginning of the world. I was hungry, you gave me food; I was thirsty, and you gave me drink; I was a stranger, and you took me in;

naked, and you clothed me; I was sick, and you visited me; I was in prison, and you came to me.'

"Then the righteous ones will ask him, Lord, when did we find you hungry, and feed you? Or thirsty, and give you a drink? When did we meet you as a stranger, and take you in? Or naked, and clothe you? Or when did we see you sick, or in prison, and come to you?' The King will answer them: 'Here's the truth: Insofar as you have done it to one of the least of my brothers and sisters, you have done it to me.'

"Then he will say to those on the left, 'You are cursed. Get away from me, go into the everlasting fire which is prepared for the devil and his angels. I was hungry, and you gave me no food. I was thirsty, and you gave me no drink. I was a stranger, and you did not take me in; naked, and you did not clothe me; sick, and in prison, and you did not visit me.'

"Then they will also ask him: 'Lord, when did we see you hungry, or thirsty, or a stranger, or naked, or sick, or in prison, and did not help you? He will answer them, 'Here is the truth: Insofar as you didn't do these things to one of the least of my brothers and sisters, you did not do it to me.' These will go away into everlasting punishment. But the righteous will go into eternal life."

When Jesus finished speaking, he said to his disciples, "You know that the feast of the Passover is in two days. Then the Son of Man will be betrayed and crucified." The chief priests, the scribes, and the elders of the people gathered together at the high priest's palace. His name was Caiaphas. They consulted with him about how they could discreetly take Jesus and kill him. They said, "Let's not do it on the feast day or there may be an uproar among the people."

Then Satan got into Judas Iscariot, who was one of the twelve disciples. And he went on his way and conspired with the chief priests and captains to figure out how he could betray Jesus to them. He said, "What will you give me if I will deliver him to you?" When they heard this, they were glad. They made a deal with him for thirty pieces of silver. Judas

Judas Joins the Conspiracy

Matt. 26:1–5, 14-16
Mark 14:1-2, 10-11
Luke 22:1-6

promised to do it and began to look for an opportunity to betray Jesus to them, somewhere away from the crowds.

Peter and John
Prepare the
Last Meal

Matt. 26:17-19
Mark 14:12-16
Luke 22:7-13

The day of unleavened bread was coming. This is when the Passover sacrifice would be killed. Jesus' disciples asked him, "Where do you want us to go to prepare to eat the Passover?" He sent Peter and John and told them, "Go and prepare the Passover meal for us.

"Look, when you entered the city, a man bearing a pitcher of water will meet you. Follow him into the house he enters, and say to the owner of the house, 'The Master says, "My time is at hand; where is the guest room where I will eat the Passover with my disciples?"'" He will show you a large, furnished, upstairs room. Prepare the meal there." And so they went, and found everything to be as he had said. And they made ready for the Passover.

A Final
Gathering

• The Foot-
washing

John 13:1-20

Before the Passover meal, Jesus knew that the time had come for him to leave this world and go to the Father (he had loved his own, the ones in the world, and he loved them to the end). Supper was over (the devil had already put the idea of betrayal into the heart of Judas Iscariot, Simon's son), and Jesus knew that the Father had given him everything, also that he had come from God, and would go to God. So Jesus got up from the supper table, removed his clothes, took a towel, and wrapped it around himself. Then he poured water into a basin and began to wash the disciples' feet, wiping them with the towel.

When he came to Simon Peter, Peter said to him, "Lord, why do you wash my feet?" Jesus answered, "Right now you don't know why I do this. But you will understand later." Peter said to him, "You will never wash my feet." Jesus answered him, "If I do not wash you, you won't belong to me." Simon Peter said, "Lord, wash not only my feet, but also my hands and my head!"

Jesus said, "Whoever has already washed his body only needs his feet washed to be clean all over. And you are clean. But this is not true of everyone here." Jesus knew who would betray him.

This is why he said, "You are not all clean." So after he had washed their feet, had gotten dressed, and sat down again at the table, he said to them, "Do you know what I have done to you?

"You call me 'Teacher' and 'Lord.' And this is true, because that is what I am. If I am your Lord and teacher, and have washed your feet, you should also wash each other's feet. I have given you this as an example, so that you should do just as I have done. I tell you the truth, the servant is not greater than his lord; nor is the one who is sent greater than the sender. You know these things and will be blessed if you do them. I am not speaking to you all. I know whom I have chosen. The words of the Scripture must come true: 'He that eats bread with me has turned against me.'

"Now I will tell you what is going to happen so that, when it happens, you will believe that I am Christ. Listen to the truth: Those who receive the ones I send, receive me. Those who receive me, receive the one who sent me."

Matt. 26:20-25
Mark 14:17-20
Luke 22:21-23
John 13:21-30

When Jesus said this, he was troubled in his spirit. As they were eating, he testified, "Here is the truth, one of you will betray me. He is with me at the table." Then the disciples looked at each other, wondering whom he was talking about. And they were exceedingly sorrowful, and every one of them began to say to him, "Lord, is it I?" One of Jesus' disciples, whom Jesus loved, was sitting near him at the table. Simon Peter signaled to him to ask whom Jesus was talking about. This disciple asked him, "Lord, who is it?"

Jesus answered, "It is the one to whom I will give bit of bread dipped in the sauce. The Son of Man will go in the way the Scriptures say. But woe to the man who betrays the Son of Man! It would be better for that man if he had not been born." Then Judas, who betrayed him, asked, "Master, is it I?" He said to him, "You have said it." And he dipped the bread and gave it to Judas Iscariot.

After Judas ate the bread, Satan entered into him, and Jesus said to him, "Do what you must do quickly." None of the men at the table knew why Jesus had said this to Judas. Some of them thought it was because Judas took care of the money. So they thought Jesus was telling him to buy some things they needed for the Passover feast. Or perhaps that he should give something to the poor. Nevertheless, after Judas ate the dipped bread, he immediately went out into the night.

When he was gone, Jesus said, "Now the Son of Man is glorified, and so God is glorified in him. Since God is glorified in him, God will immediately glorify him in himself.

• The
Lord's Table

Matt. 26:26-29
Mark 14:21-25
Luke 22:14-20

When the time came, he sat down with the apostles and said to them, "I have always wanted to eat the Passover with you before I suffer. Listen to me, I will not eat this meal again until it is fully realized in the kingdom of God."

As they were eating, Jesus took some bread, blessed it, broke it, gave it to the disciples, and said, "Take, and eat this; it is my body given for you. Do this in remembrance of me." After supper, he took a cup of wine, gave thanks, gave it to them, and said, "Drink all of this wine. It is the token of my blood—the blood of the new covenant, which I will pour out to discharge the sins of many people."

A disagreement arose among the disciples: Which of them would be the greatest of all in the coming kingdom? Jesus said to them, "The kings of this world rule the people, yet the same people call them 'patrons.' But you will not be like this. Instead, the greatest among you will take the lowest place. The chief is the one who will serve the others. Consider this, who is greater, the one that sits down to eat, or the one that serves the meal? Isn't it the one who sits and eats? But I am here serving you.

"You have remained with me through all my trials. And my Father has given a kingdom to me. You will eat and drink at my table in that kingdom, and sit on thrones to judge the twelve tribes of Israel.

Little children, I'll be with you for a little while longer. Then you will look for me. And, as I told the Jewish leaders, you

• Love and Denial

Luke 22:31-38
John 13:33-38

cannot come where I am going. So I give you this new commandment: Love one another just as I have loved you. When you do this, all people will know that you are my disciples; that is, if you love one another."

Simon Peter said, "Lord, where are you going?" Jesus answered, "Now you cannot follow me where I am going. But you will follow me later." Peter said, "Lord, why can't I follow you now? I will lay down my life for you." Jesus answered, "Will you lay down your life for me? Actually, before the rooster crows, you will deny me three times.

"Simon, Simon, look! Satan wants you, so he can sift you like flour. But I have prayed that your faith would not fail. When you are changed, strengthen your brothers and sisters." Peter said to him, "Lord, I am ready to go with you into prison, and even to death." And Jesus said, "I tell you, Peter, the rooster will not crow today, before you deny that you know me three times."

Jesus said to them all, "When I sent you out without purse, money, or shoes—

did you lack anything?" They said, "Nothing." Then he said, "But now, if you have a purse, take it, and likewise money. If you don't have a sword, sell your coat and buy one. For I say that what is written about me must still be fulfilled: 'And he was counted along with the rebels.' The things the prophets said about me will come true." They said, "Lord, look, here are two swords." He said, "That's enough."

Don't worry. You believe in God, so believe in me, too. There are many rooms in my Father's house. If this weren't true, I would tell you. I will go and prepare a place for you there. Then I will come and get you so that you can be with me. You know where I am going, and you know the way as well."

Thomas said to him, "Lord, we don't know where you are going. And how can we know the way?" Jesus said to him, "I am the way, the truth, and the life; no one can come to the Father but through me. If you had known me, you would have known my Father too. From

The Final Teaching

• The Way to the Father

John 14:1-14

now on, you know him, and you have seen him."

But Philip said, "Lord, show us the Father and we will be satisfied. Jesus said to him, "Have I been with you all this time, and yet you do not know me, Philip? Whoever has seen me has seen the Father. How can you say, 'Show us the Father?' Don't you believe that I am in the Father, and the Father is in me? The words that I speak to you are not my words. They belong to the Father, who lives and works in me. Believe me, I am in the Father, and the Father is in me. Or at least believe me because of all the things you have seen me do.

"Here is the truth: Whoever believes in me will do the same works that I do and will do even greater works than these. Why? Because I am going to be with my Father. So whatever you ask in my name, I will do. Then the Father will be glorified in the Son. Remember, ask anything in my name, and I will do it!

If you love me, keep my commandments. And I will pray to the Father, and he will give you another Comforter. He will live with you forever. He is the Spirit of truth whom the world cannot receive. It cannot see him or know him. But you know him because he lives with you now, and will soon be in you. I will not leave you like orphans. I will come to you.

"In a little while, the world will see me no more. But you see me, and because I live, you will also live. On that day you will know that I am in my Father, you are in me, and I am in you. Those who keep my commandments are the ones who love me. And my Father will love those who love me; and I will love them, and will reveal myself to each of them."

Judas (not Iscariot) asked him, "Lord, how will you reveal yourself to us and not to the world?" Jesus answered, "If a man loves me, he will keep my words. Then my Father will love him, we will come to him, and make our home with him. If someone does not love me, he will not keep my words. The message you hear is not mine; it is from the Father who sent me.

• The Coming of the Spirit

Matt. 26:30
John 14:15-31

"I have spoken these things to you while I am still with you. But the Comforter, the Holy Spirit (whom the Father will send in my name) will teach you everything and will cause you to remember everything I have said to you. I leave peace with you; I give my peace to you and it is not like what the world gives. Don't let your heart be troubled or afraid.

"You've heard me say, 'I'm going away and coming again to you.' If you love me, you will rejoice for me, because I am going to the Father, who is greater than I am. And I have told you about this before it happens, so that, when it does happen, you will believe. I will not talk much with you from now on, because the prince of this world approaches, and he has no power over me. But I will do as the Father has instructed so that the world may know that I love the Father. Come, let's go." Then they sang a hymn and went out to the Mount of Olives.

Thursday

The Final
Teaching
(continued)

I am the real vine. My Father is the farmer. He cuts off every branch in the vine that does not bear fruit. And every branch that does bear fruit, he prunes so that it may bring forth even more. You have already been pruned through the message which I have given to you.

• The Fruit of Abiding in God

John 15:1-16

"Remain in me, and I will remain in you. A branch cannot bear fruit by itself. It must remain in the vine. The same applies to you: Remain in me and bear fruit. I am the vine, you are the branches. Those who remain in me, and I in them will bring forth much fruit. Outside of me you can do nothing. If a person does not remain in me, he is thrown away and withers. Men gather such branches, throw them into the fire, and they are burned. If you remain in me, and my words remain in you, you can ask me for whatever you want, and it will be given to you.

"When you, my disciples, bear fruit, my Father is glorified. The Father has loved me; in the same way, I have loved you. Remain in my love. If you keep my commandments, you will remain in my love, just as I have kept my Father's commandments, and remain in his love. I have told you these things that my joy may remain in you, and so that your joy would be full.

"This is my commandment: Love one another, as I have loved you. No one has greater love than this: to lay down his life for his friends. You are my friends if you do what I command. From now on, I will not call you 'servants.' Why? Because a servant does not know what his master is doing. I have called you friends because I have told you everything that I have heard from my Father. You have not chosen me, I chose you, and commissioned you to go out and bring forth lasting fruit and whatever you ask from the Father in my name, he will give it to you.

• The
World's
Hatred

John 15:17-16:4

I command you to love one another. If the world hates you, remember that it hated me before it hated you. If you were a part of the world, the world would love you. You are not a part of the world, because I have chosen you out of the world. So the world hates you.

"Remember what I said, 'The servant is not greater than his lord.' Since they have persecuted me, they will certainly persecute you. If they had listened to me, they would listen to you too. But they will persecute and ignore you because you are mine, and because they do know not the Father who sent me. If I had not come and spoken to them, they would not be guilty. But now they cannot cover their sin. Whoever hates me hates my Father too.

"If I had not done things among them which no other man could do, they would not be guilty. But they saw all I have done and still they hate me and my Father. But this has happened to fulfill the words written in their own law: 'They hated me without a cause.' But I will send the Comforter, the Spirit of truth, to you from the Father and he will testify about me. You also will be my witnesses, because you have been with me from the beginning.

"I have told you these things so that you will not be surprised when they throw you out of the synagogues. Yes, the time is coming when those who kill you will think that they are serving God. They will do this to you because they have not known me or the Father. I tell you this so that when the time comes, you will remember my warning. I haven't told you before this because we still had plenty of time to be together.

But now I am going away to the one who sent me, and none of you has asked, 'Where are you going?' Instead you are full of sorrow about the things I've told you. Nevertheless, it is best for you that I go away. Yes, it's true. If I don't go away, the Comforter will not come to you. But if I depart, I will send him to you.

"When he comes, he will convince the world of its sin, of God's righteousness, and of the coming judgment. The world's sin is that they do not believe in me. But God's righteousness is available because I go to my Father, and you will no longer see me. Judgment will come because the prince of this world has already been judged.

"I have many more things to say to you, but you cannot bear any more for now. However, when the Spirit of truth comes, he will lead you into the truth. He will not speak his own ideas. Instead, whatever he hears, he will speak. He will tell you about the future. He will glorify me, because he will only reveal to you the things he receives from me. All things that belong to the Father are mine. This is why

I said that the Spirit will reveal to you the things he receives from me. In a little while you will not see me. Then, a little while later, you will see me again. Because I am going to the Father."

• The Joy of Childbirth

John 16:17-33

Some of his disciples said to each other, "What is he saying, 'In a little while you will not see me. Then, a little while later, you will see me again'? and 'Because I am going to the Father'? What does this mean, 'A little while'? We don't know what he is talking about!"

Jesus knew what they wanted to ask him, and said, "Are you asking each other what I mean by 'In a little while you will not see me. Then, a little while later, you will see me again'? Truthfully, you will weep and lament over what is about to happen to me, but the world will rejoice. You will be sorrowful, but your sorrow will turn to joy.

"A pregnant woman is in pain when her labor begins, because the time to deliver her child has come. But as soon as the baby is born, her pain is changed to joy because her child is born into the world. You have sorrow now. But I will see you again, and your heart will rejoice. No one will be able to take away that joy.

"When that day comes, you will no longer have to ask me anything. In fact, whatever you ask the Father in my name, he will give you. Up to now you have not asked in my name. So ask, you will receive, and you will be full of joy.

"I have used parables to describe these things to you. But soon this will not be necessary. Instead, I will tell you plainly about the Father. From then on, you will ask the Father in my name. I am not saying that I will ask the Father for you. The Father loves you because you love me, and believe that I came from God. Yes, I came from the Father into the world. And now I leave the world and go back to the Father."

His disciples said to him, "Finally! You're using plain words instead of parables. Now we understand that you know everything. No one needs to tell you anything. This is why we believe that you came from God."

Jesus asked, "Do you finally believe?

Look, the time is near. In fact, the time has come when you will be scattered. Everyone will go his own way and leave me all alone. Yet I am not alone. The Father is with me. I have told you all these things so that you will have peace in me. In the world you will have tribulation. But be of good cheer—I have overcome the world."

After Jesus said this, he lifted his eyes up to heaven, and said, "Father, the time is come—glorify your Son so that your Son can return the glory to you. You have given him authority over all the people on earth so he can give eternal life to everyone you have given him. And this is eternal life: To know you, the only true God, and Jesus Christ, whom you have sent. I have glorified you on the earth. I have finished the work which you gave me to do. And now, O Father, glorify me in yourself with the glory I had with you before the world was made.

I have revealed you to the men whom you gave to me out of the world. They were yours, and you gave them to me. And they

The Final Prayer

• For Himself

John 17:1-5

• For the Disciples

John 17:6-19

have kept your word. Now they know that all the things you have given me are really yours, because I have given them the message that you gave me. They have received the message, and know with certainty that I came from you. They believe that you sent me.

"I pray, not for the world, but for these whom you gave me—they are yours. They are mine so they are yours, and all the people that belong to you are mine as well. I am glorified in them. Now I am no longer in the world, I come to you. But these men remain here in the world. Holy Father, keep them through your own name—all these you have given to me—so that they may be united as one just like you and me. When I was with them in the world, I kept them in your name—none of them was lost except the son of damnation so that the Scripture would be fulfilled.

"Now I am coming to you. I have told them all these things so that they would be filled with my joy. I delivered to them your message. The world hates them, because, like me, they are not a part of the world.

I'm not asking that you would take them out of the world, but that you would keep them from the evil one. They are not part of this world any more than I am.

"Purify them through your truth—your word is truth. Just as you sent me into the world, so I have sent them into the world. For their sakes I purify myself, so that they also would be made pure through the truth.

Nor do I pray only for these men—but also for the ones who will believe in me through their words. I ask that they all may be one—just as you, Father, are in me, and I in you—that they also may be one in us. Then the world will believe that you sent me. I have given them the glory that you gave to me so that they may be one, even as we are one—I in them, and you in me—that they may be perfected into one that the world may know that you sent me, and have loved them just as you have loved me.

"Father, I ask that all the people whom you have given me would be with me where I am, and that they would see the

• For All Believers

John 17:20-26

glory which you have given to me. Because you loved me before the world began. O righteous Father! The world does not know you. But I know you, and these people know that you sent me. I have told them who you are, and will continue to tell them this so that your love for me will be in them, and I in them."

In a Place
Called
Gethsemane

• His Agony

Matt 26:30-46
Mark 14:26-42
Luke 22:39-46
John 18:1-2

Jesus and his disciples sang a hymn and went out of the city to the Mount of Olives. They crossed the Kidron valley to a garden, a place called Gethsemane. Judas (who betrayed him) knew the place well, because Jesus often went there with his disciples.

Jesus said to them, "All you will be troubled because of me this night. Why? Because it is written in Scripture, 'Strike down the shepherd, and the sheep will be scattered.' But after I rise from the dead, I will go before you into Galilee."

Peter said to him, "Even if everyone else is disturbed, I won't be." Jesus said to him, "Listen, tonight, before the rooster crows, you will deny me three times." But Peter insisted, "Even if I have to die with you, I will not deny you." The rest of the disciples said the same thing.

Then Jesus said to the disciples, "Sit here, while I go over there to pray. "He took along Peter and the two sons of Zebedee. Then his heart became sorrowful and very heavy and he said to them, "My soul is more than sorrowful; it is like death. Stay here and pray with me." He went a little farther on, fell on his face, and prayed like this: "O my Father, Abba Father! If it is possible, let this cup pass from me. Nevertheless don't do what I want, do what you will." An angel appeared from heaven and strengthened him. He was in agony and so prayed more gravely and his sweat was almost like big drops of blood falling on the ground.

He came back to the disciples and found them asleep. He said to Peter, "What? Couldn't you pray with me for one hour? Watch and pray, so that you are not tempted. Your spirit is willing, but your flesh is weak."

He went a second time and prayed, "O my Father! If I cannot avoid drinking this cup, your will be done." He came back and found them asleep again. They were very tired. So he left them there, went away again, and prayed for the third time, with the same words. Then he came to his disciples, and said, "Sleep on now, take your rest. Look, the time has come—the Son of Man is betrayed to the sinners. Rise up, let's go. Look, the man who is going to betray me is here."

• His Arrest

Matt. 26:47-56
Mark 14:43-52
Luke 22:47-53
John 18:3-11

While he was still speaking, Judas, one of the twelve, came from the chief priests and elders of the people. With him came a crowd of men with swords and spears, lanterns and torches, and other weapons. Judas told them that he would betray Jesus to them with a certain signal: "Whomever I kiss, that is Jesus. Grab him."

Jesus knew everything that would happen to him. He went out of the garden, and said to the crowd, "Whom are you looking for?" They answered, "Jesus of Nazareth." Jesus said to them, "I am he." And Judas (who betrayed him), stood among them. When Jesus said, "I am he," they stepped back and fell to the ground. Then he asked again, "Whom are you looking for?" They said, "Jesus of Nazareth." Jesus answered, "I've told you that I am he. If you are looking for me, let these men go on their way." This fulfilled the Scripture which says, "I have lost none of those you gave me."

Judas came to Jesus and said, "Hello, master," and kissed him. "Jesus said to him, "Friend, why have you come? Do you betray the Son of Man with a kiss?" Then they grabbed Jesus, and took him. One of the disciples drew his sword, and struck the high priest's servant and cut off his ear. The servant's name was Malchus. Jesus touched the man's ear, healed him, and said, "That's enough. Put away your sword —they that use a sword will die by the sword. Don't you think, right now, I could pray to my Father, and he would send me more than twelve legions of angels? But if I did, how would the Scriptures be fulfilled? It must happen like this. Shouldn't I drink the cup that my Father has given me?"

Then Jesus spoke to the crowd, "Why have you come out with swords and spears to take me like I am a thief? Every day I sat with you teaching in the temple, and you didn't arrest me. But this is your time, and the power of darkness." All this happened so that the writings of the prophets could be fulfilled. Then all the disciples abandoned him, and ran. One of Jesus' followers was a young man wearing a linen cloth wrapped around his naked body. The young men in the crowd grabbed him, he twisted out of the linen cloth, and ran away naked.

His Condemnation by Religious Leaders

• Annas, the High Priest

John 18:12-24

Then the band and the captain and officers of the Jews took Jesus, tied him up, and led him away to Annas, the father-in-law of Caiaphas, who was the high priest that year. (Caiaphas was the one who advised the Jewish leaders that it was best for one man to die for the people.)

Simon Peter followed Jesus, as did another disciple. The high priest knew that disciple, and so he went with Jesus into the high priest's palace. But Peter stood outside the door. Then the disciple who knew the high priest spoke to the young woman who was the doorkeeper, and brought Peter inside. The woman who kept the door said to Peter, "Aren't you one of this man's disciples?" Peter said, "I am not."

The servants and officers had made a fire out of coal because it was cold. As they warmed themselves, Peter stood with them and warmed himself too.

The high priest asked Jesus about his disciples and his doctrine. Jesus answered, "I spoke openly to the world. I taught in the synagogue, in the temple, wherever Jews were. I said nothing in secret. Why do you ask me? Instead, ask those who heard me about what I said to them. Certainly they know what I said." When he said this, one of the officers who stood by struck Jesus with the palm of his hand, and demanded, "Do you answer the high priest like this?" Jesus answered, "If I have spoken something evil, say what the evil is. But if I speak the truth, why do you strike me?" So Annas sent him, tied up, to Caiaphas the high priest.

They led Jesus away to the house of Caiaphas, the high priest, where the scribes and the elders were gathered. Peter followed from afar, went in the courtyard,

• Caiaphas, the High Priest

Matt. 26:57-68
Mark 14:53-65

warmed himself at the fire, and sat with the servants, to see the end of it all.

The chief priests, elders, and all the council, looked for people who would lie about Jesus so they could put him to death; but they were unsuccessful. Yes, many witnesses came and lied about him, but the things they said did not agree. At last, two witnesses came and said, "This fellow said, 'I am able to destroy the temple of God, and to build it in three days.' " The high priest stood up and said to Jesus, "Don't you have anything to say about what these witnesses say against you?"

Jesus said nothing. And the high priest said to him, "I appeal to you by the living God, that you tell us whether or not you are the Christ, the Son of God." Jesus said to him, "You have said it. Nevertheless, I say to you, after this you will see the Son of Man sitting at the right side of God, and coming in the clouds from heaven."

The high priest tore his clothes, saying, "He has spoken blasphemy! What further proof do we need? Look! You have all heard his blasphemy. What do you think?" They answered, "He is guilty of death!" And some spit on him, covered his face, and shoved him around the room. Others slapped him with the palms of their hands, saying, "Prophesy to us, you Christ. Who slapped you?"

Then they took him into the high priest's house. Peter followed from afar. A fire was kindled in the midst of the hall; they sat down there together, and Peter sat among them. One of the maids of the high priest said to him, "You were with Jesus of Galilee." But he denied this before them all, "I don't know what you are talking about." He went out onto the porch. The rooster crowed. Another maid saw him, and said to the others, "This fellow was with Jesus of Nazareth." Again he denied this with an oath, "I do not know the man."

After a while some who stood by came and said to Peter, "Surely you are one of them. You are a Galilean, we can tell by the accent of your speech." Peter cursed, "I do not know the man." The rooster crowed a second time. And the Lord turned, and looked at Peter. Then Peter remembered what Jesus had said: "You will deny me

• A Disciple's Denial

Matt. 26:69-75
Mark 14:66-72
Luke 22:54-65
John 18:25-27

three times before the rooster crows twice." When he thought about this, he went out and bitterly wept.

Friday

The Religious Condemnation Continues

• The Religious Council

Matt. 27:1-2
Mark 15:1
Luke 22:66-71

When morning came, all the chief priests and elders of the people deliberated about how to put Jesus to death. They brought him in and said, "Are you the Christ? Tell us." He answered, "If I tell you, you will not believe. And if I ask you what you think about this, you will not answer me or let me go. After this, the Son of Man will sit on the right side of the power of God."

Then they all demanded, "Are you the Son of God?" He answered, "You say that I am." They said, "Do we need any further proof? We have heard it from his own mouth." They tied him up, led him away, and delivered him to Pontius Pilate, the Roman governor.

• The Betrayer Is Betrayed

Matt. 27:3-10

When Judas (who betrayed him) saw that Jesus was condemned to die, he changed his mind and brought the thirty pieces of silver back to the chief priests and elders. "I have sinned," he said. "I have betrayed an innocent man." They said, "So what? That's your problem."

Judas threw the silver down on the temple floor, went out, and hanged himself. The chief priests took the silver pieces, and said, "It is not lawful to put this into the treasury because it is the price paid for murder." So they deliberated, and decided to use the silver to buy the potter's field for use as a pauper's graveyard. This is why that field is called the Field of Blood to this day. This fulfilled the words of Jeremiah the prophet, who said, "And they took the thirty pieces of silver, the amount of his value to the children of Israel, and gave them to purchase the potter's field, as the Lord advised."

The whole crowd arose, and led Jesus from Caiaphas's house to the hall of judgment. It was still early, but they did not go into the judgment hall, so that they would not be defiled and be unable to legally eat the Passover meal. So Pilate went outside to see them, and said, "What accusation do you bring against this man?" They answered, "If he were not a criminal, we would not have brought him to you. We

His Condemnation by Politicians

• Pilate, the Governor

Matt. 27:11-14
Mark 15:2-5
Luke 23:1-5
John 18:28-38

found this fellow leading the nation astray, and discouraging the people from paying taxes to Caesar. He says that he is Christ, a King."

Jesus stood in front of Pilate, and the governor asked him, "Are you the King of the Jews?" Jesus said, "It is just as you say." And when he was accused by the chief priests and elders, he said nothing. Then Pilate said to him, "Don't you hear the things they say against you?" Jesus answered not a word, and the governor was quite surprised at this.

Then Pilate said to the chief priests and the people, "I find no fault in this man. You take him. Judge him according to your own law." But the Jewish leaders said to him, "It is not legal for us to execute a man." This fulfilled Jesus' own words about the way he would be put to death. Then they became even more fierce, and said, "He stirs up the people with his teaching all the way from Galilee to this very place."

Then Pilate returned into the judgment hall, called Jesus, and said to him, "Are you the King of the Jews?" Jesus answered, "Is this your own question, or did others tell you to ask me this?" Pilate answered, "Am I a Jew? Your own nation and its chief priests have brought you to me. What have you done?" Jesus answered, "My kingdom is not in this world. If it were, then my followers would fight, and not allow me to be arrested by the Jews. But my kingdom is not of this world."

So Pilate said to him, "Are you a king then?" Jesus answered, "You say that I am a king and you are right. This is why I was born. I came to bring truth into the world and everyone who loves the truth hears my voice. Pilate said to him, "What is truth?" After he said this, he went out again to the Jews, and said to them, "I find no fault in him at all."

When Pilate heard the Jewish leaders mention Galilee, he asked if Jesus was a Galilean. Since this region was a part of Herod's territory, Pilate sent Jesus to Herod, who happened to be in Jerusalem at that time.

• Herod, the King

Luke 23:6-12

Herod was very glad that Jesus was sent to him. He had wanted to see him for a long time—he had heard so many things about him. He hoped to see Jesus do some kind of miracle.

Herod questioned Jesus in detail, but Jesus did not answer him. Still the chief priests and scribes viciously accused him. So Herod and his soldiers ridiculed and mocked Jesus, wrapped him in a gorgeous robe, and sent him back to Pilate. From then on Pilate and Herod were fast friends, although before this they had been enemies.

• Pilate, the Priests, and the Festival Crowd

Matt. 27:15-26
Mark 15:6-15
Luke 23:13-25
John 18:39-
    19:16

There the soldiers braided a crown of thorns, and put it on his head. They put a purple robe on him, and shouted, "Hail, King of the Jews!" and hit him with their hands. Then Pilate went out again, and said to them, "Look, here he is. I want you to know that I find no fault in him." Then Jesus came out, wearing the crown of thorns and the purple robe. Pilate said, "Look at this man!"

When the chief priests and officers saw him, they cried out, "Crucify him, crucify him!" Pilate said to them, "You take him and crucify him yourselves, because I find no fault in him." The Jewish leaders answered him, "We have a law that says he should die because he says he is the Son of God." When Pilate heard this, he was even more afraid.

He went back into the judgment hall, and said to Jesus, "Who are you?" But Jesus did not answer. Then Pilate said to him, "You won't speak to me? Don't you know that I have the power to either crucify you or set you free?" Jesus answered, "You could have no power over me if it wasn't given to you from God. The real sinners are those who have brought me here to you."

So Pilate wanted to release him. But the Jewish leaders cried out, "If you let this man go, you are not Caesar's friend! Whoever says he is a king speaks against Caesar." When Pilate heard this, he brought Jesus outside, sat down on the judgment seat in the place called the Pavement. (In Aramaic it is called Gabbatha.) When he was settled in the judgment seat, his wife sent word to him, "Leave that righteous man alone. I had an awful nightmare about him last night."

It was the day for the preparation of the Passover feast. At about noon, Pilate said to the Jews, "Look, your King!" But they cried out, "Away with him, away with him! Crucify him!" Pilate said, "Should I crucify your King?" The chief priests answered, "Our only king is Caesar."

It was the governor's custom to release a prisoner during the feast. There was an important prisoner at that time called Barabbas. He had been arrested with his followers while leading an insurrection during which he had committed a murder. The crowd cried out loudly asking him to release a prisoner as he had always done. Pilate asked them, "Whom do you want me to release? Barabbas, or Jesus, called Christ, the King of the Jews?" (He knew that the chief priests had arrested Jesus out of envy.)

The chief priests and elders persuaded the crowd to ask that Barabbas be freed and that Jesus be executed. The governor answered them, "Which of the two do you want me to release?" And they said, "Barabbas." Pilate said to them, "What should I do with Jesus, called Christ?"

They all said to him, "Let him be crucified." And the governor said, "Why, what has he done wrong?" But they cried out even more, "Let him be crucified!"

Pilate saw that he could do nothing more. So, to prevent a riot, he took water, washed his hands so they all could see, and said, "I am innocent of the death of this righteous man. You are responsible." Then all the people said, "Yes, we and our children will bear the responsibility for his death." Then Pilate released Barabbas, had Jesus whipped, and sent him to be crucified.

Then the governor's soldiers took Jesus into the common hall, called the Praetorium. They all gathered around him, stripped him, and put a scarlet robe on him. They braided a crown of thorns, and put it upon his head. They put a stick in his right hand, bowed down before him, and mocked him, saying, "Hail, King of the Jews!" They spit upon him, took the stick and hit him on the head. And after they had mocked him, they took off the robe, and put his own clothes on him, and

• The Roman Soldiers

Matt. 27:27-31
Mark 15:16-20

led him away to crucify him.

His Crucifixion

• He Walks
to Golgotha

Matt. 27:32-34
Mark 15:21-23
Luke 23:26-31
John 19:17

As they led him away, they seized Simon, a Cyrenian (the father of Alexander and Rufus), who had come to the city from the country. They put the cross on his shoulder and he carried it, following behind Jesus. A great crowd of people, including women, followed him wailing and lamenting for him.

Jesus turned to them and said, "Daughters of Jerusalem, don't weep for me. Instead weep for yourselves, and for your children. Because the time is coming when they will say, 'Blessed are all women who have never borne children and fed them from their breast.' Then they will say to the mountains, 'Fall on us!' and to the hills, 'Cover us!' Think of it: if they do this when the fig tree is green, what will they do when it is dry?"

When they came to a place called Golgotha (this means Skull Hill), they offered him vinegar to drink, drugged with myrrh. When he tasted it, he would not drink it.

At nine in the morning, they crucified him. The soldiers took his clothes away and divided them four ways. When they looked at his robe, which was woven in one piece from the top to the bottom, they said among themselves, "Let's not tear it; let's gamble to decide who will get it." This fulfilled these words of Scripture: "They divided my clothes among them, and for my robe, they cast lots."

• He Hangs on a Cross

Matt. 27:35-44
Mark 15:24-32
Luke 23:32-43
John 19:18-27

They sat down and watched him. Posted over his head was the accusation, THIS IS JESUS OF NAZARETH, THE KING OF THE JEWS. Many of the Jewish leaders saw this, because the place where Jesus was crucified was near the city. The accusation was written in Hebrew, and Greek, and Latin. The chief priests said to Pilate, "Don't write 'The King of the Jews.' Instead write, 'He said, I am King of the Jews.' Pilate replied, "I have written what I have written."

Two thieves were crucified there with him, one on the right, and another on the left. And so the Scripture was fulfilled which says, "He was counted with the transgressors."

Jesus said, "Father, forgive them; because they do not know what they are doing." Those who passed by berated him, shaking their heads, saying, "You said you would destroy the temple, and build it again in three days. So save yourself. If you are the Son of God, come down from the cross." The chief priests did the same and mocked him, together with the scribes and elders: "He saved others, but he cannot save himself. If he is the King of Israel, let him come down from the cross, then we will believe him. He trusted in God; let God save him now. That is, if God wants him, after all, he said, 'I am the Son of God.'" The thieves who were crucified with him also reviled him.

And one of these criminals railed at Jesus: "If you are the Christ, save yourself and save us too." But the other criminal rebuked him, "Don't you fear God? You share the same punishment as this man. We deserve to be punished for what we did. But this man has done nothing wrong." Then he said to Jesus, "Lord, remember me when you come into your kingdom." Jesus said to him, "I am telling you the truth, today you will be with me in paradise."

There by the cross of Jesus stood his mother, his mother's sister, Mary the wife of Clopas, and Mary Magdalene. When Jesus saw his mother and the disciple whom he loved standing nearby, he said to his mother, "Woman, here is your son!" Then he said to the disciple, "There is your mother!" From that day on, that disciple took Jesus' mother into his own home.

Beginning at noon until three o'clock, there was darkness over all the land. At about three, Jesus cried with a loud voice, "Eli, Eli, lama sabachthani?" This means, "My God, my God, why have you left me alone?" Some of the people standing there heard this, and said, "This man calls for Elijah." Immediately one of them ran, took a sponge, filled it with vinegar, put it on a stick, and gave it to Jesus to drink. The rest of them said, "Let him be. Let's see whether Elijah will come to save him."

After this, Jesus knew that all things were complete. When he had taken the vinegar, he cried again with a loud voice,

• He Dies

Matt. 27:45-56
Mark 15:33-41
Luke 23:44-49
John 19:28-37

"It is finished. Father, I entrust my spirit to your hands." After he said this, he bowed his head and gave up his spirit. Just then, the veil of the temple was torn in two from the top to the bottom. The earth shook, rocks cracked, and graves opened. After his resurrection, many bodies of the dead believers arose from their graves and went into the holy city, where many people saw them.

The officer of the guard, and those with him, were watching Jesus. They saw the earthquake, and all that happened and were very afraid. "He really was the Son of God," they said. The people who came to watch these crucifixions saw all the things that happened, and returned into the city in mourning.

But Jesus' friends, and many women who had followed Jesus from Galilee, ministering to his needs, watched from far off. Among these was Mary Magdalene, Mary the mother of James and Joseph, the mother of Zebedee's children, and many other women who had traveled with him to Jerusalem.

It was the day of preparation for the

Sabbath and the Jewish leaders didn't want the bodies to remain upon the crosses on the Sabbath day, so they asked Pilate to have a soldier break the prisoners' legs. Then they would die quickly and could be taken away. The soldiers broke the legs of the two men who were crucified with Jesus. But when they came to Jesus, they saw that he was already dead. So they did not break his legs. But one of the soldiers stabbed him in the side with a spear, and out of the wound came blood and water.

This is an accurate eyewitness report. It is presented here so that you can believe. All these things were done to fulfill the words of Scripture: "Not one of his bones will be broken," and "They will look on him whom they pierced."

In the evening, a rich man, one of Jesus' followers who was waiting for the coming of the kingdom of God, came to the place. He was named Joseph and was an honored member of the Jewish high council from the town of Arimathea. (He did not agree with the council's decision to put Jesus to death.) In fear of the Jewish leaders, Joseph

• He Is Buried

Matt. 27:57-61
Mark 15:42-47
Luke 23:50-56
John 19:38-42

went to Pilate secretly and asked for the body of Jesus. Pilate was amazed to hear that Jesus was already dead. He called the officer of the guard to ascertain whether he was dead. The officer confirmed it and so Pilate gave the body to Joseph.

Nicodemus, the man who first came to Jesus by night, brought one hundred pounds of a mixture of myrrh and aloe. They took Jesus' body and wrapped it in linen cloth with the spices in the way of Jewish burial. Then they laid the body in Joseph's own new tomb, cut out of the rock, rolled a large stone over the tomb's opening for the door, and went away. Mary Magdalene, and the other Mary, the mother of Joseph, were sitting nearby. They saw where the tomb was located and that Jesus' body was laid in it. So they returned to the city, prepared spices and ointments; and rested on the Sabbath just as the law commanded.

Saturday

Soldiers Guard His Tomb

Matt. 27:62-66

The day following the day of preparation for the Sabbath, the chief priests and Pharisees came to Pilate and said, "Sir, we remember that while that deceiver was still alive, he said, 'After three days I will rise again.' Therefore, order that his tomb be guarded until the third day, so that his disciples won't come in the night, steal his body, and then tell the people, 'He is risen from the dead.' If this happens, we will be worse off than we were before he died." Pilate said to them, "Take guards and make the tomb as secure as you can." So they put a seal on the stone at the door, and posted guards at the tomb.

Epilogue

His Resurrection, and Ascension

The Sabbath was over and it began to dawn toward the first day of the week. Mary Magdalene, the other Mary, Salome, and others came to see the tomb, bringing spices they had prepared. They said to each other, "Who will help us roll away the stone from the door of the tomb? Just then, there was a big earthquake. The angel of the Lord came down from heaven, rolled back the stone from the door, and sat on it. He looked like lightning, and his clothes were as white as snow. The guards shook with fear and fell down like they were dead.

Rising from the Dead
in Jerusalem

Matt. 28:1-15
Mark 16:1-8
Luke 24:1-12
John 20:1-9

The angel said to the women, "Don't be afraid. I know you are looking for Jesus who was crucified. Why are you seeking someone who is living in this place where everyone is dead? He is not here. He is risen, just as he said he would. Come, look at the place where the Lord lay and then go quickly, tell his disciples that he is risen from the dead, and that he has gone ahead into Galilee. You will see him there. Remember what he said to you when he was still in Galilee? He said, 'The Son of Man must be delivered into the hands of sinful men, be crucified, and on the third day rise again.' " They remembered these words, and ran away from the tomb trembling and amazed, and told these things to the eleven disciples, and to all the rest.

It was Mary Magdalene, and Joanna, and Mary the mother of James, and the other women with them, who told these things to the apostles; including Simon Peter, and to the other disciple, whom Jesus loved. They said, "They have taken the Lord out of the tomb, and we don't know where they have put him." But their words seemed to the disciples to be like idle tales, and they did not believe them. But Peter went out with the other disciple, and came to the tomb.

They ran together—though the other disciple outran Peter, and came to the tomb first. He stooped down, looked in, and saw the linen cloths lying there. Yet he did not go in. Simon Peter soon followed, went into the tomb, and saw the linen cloths, and the cloth that had been wrapped around Jesus' head. It was not lying with the linen cloths, but was folded neatly by itself.

Then the other disciple, who had arrived at the tomb first, entered, saw, and believed (though they did not yet understand the Scripture that says Jesus would rise from the dead).

When they had gone away, some of the guards went into the city and told the chief priests about all that had happened. The elders met together. Then they gave a large amount of money to the soldiers and told them, "Say that his disciples came at night, and stole his body while you were asleep. If the governor hears about it, we will stand up for you and all will be well."

So they took the money and did as they were told. The story they told is still accepted by the Jews today.

Visiting the Disciples

Speaking with Mary

Mark 16:9-11
John 20:10-18

Meanwhile, the two disciples went away to their own homes. But Mary Magdalene (the one from whom Jesus had cast seven devils), stood outside the tomb weeping. As she wept, she stooped down, looked into the tomb, and saw two angels dressed in white sitting where the body of Jesus had been. One was at the head, and the other at the feet. They said to her, "Woman, why are you weeping? She answered them, "Because they have taken my Lord away, and I do not know where they have put his body."

When she said this, she turned around and saw Jesus standing there. But she didn't know that it was Jesus. He said to her, "Woman, why are you weeping? Whom are you looking for?" She thought he was the gardener and said to him, "Sir, if you have taken him away, tell me where you have put his body and I will take it away."

Jesus said to her, "Mary." She turned,

and said to him, "Rabbi!" (which means "Master"). Jesus said to her, "Don't touch me, because I have not yet ascended to my Father. Go to my brothers, and tell them I have ascended to my Father, and your Father; to my God, and your God." Mary Magdalene told the disciples this as they mourned and wept. When they heard that he was alive, and that she had seen him, they did not believe her.

Two of the disciples traveled that same day to a village called Emmaus, seven miles from Jerusalem. On the way, they talked together about all the things that had happened. And it so happened that while they spoke, Jesus himself came near and began to walk with them. But God kept them from recognizing him.

Walking to Emmaus *near Jerusalem*

Mark 16:12-13
Luke 24:13-35

Jesus said to them, "You seem so sad as you walk along. What are you talking about?" One of them, named Cleopas, answered, "Are you a stranger in Jerusalem? Don't you know what has happened over the past few days?"

Jesus said, "What things?" They told him: "Jesus of Nazareth was a prophet recognized by God and all the people. He did powerful deeds and spoke wonderful words. The chief priests and our rulers condemned him to death, and they crucified him. We believed he was the one who would redeem Israel. Besides all this, today is the third day since these things happened.

"Yes, and some women among us, went to his tomb early this morning. When they didn't find his body, they came back to tell us that they had seen a vision of angels who said he was alive. And then some of the men among us went to the tomb, and found that what the women said was true. But they didn't see Jesus."

Then Jesus said to them, "You are foolish. Why do you find it hard to believe what the prophets have said? Didn't they say that Christ would suffer these things, and then enter into glory?" Then he explained the Scriptures to them from Moses and the prophets, and told them all the things they said about him.

They came near the village where they were going, and he seemed to be going on his way. But they convinced him not to go. "Stay with us. It is evening; the day is almost over." And so he went in with them.

And then, as he sat eating with them, he took bread, blessed it, broke it, and gave to them. Suddenly they realized who he was; and just then he vanished. They said to each other, "Didn't our hearts feel warm while he talked with us along the road and explained the Scriptures to us?"

Within the hour, the two left to return to Jerusalem. They came to where the eleven disciples were gathered together and were told, "The Lord is really risen! He has appeared to Simon." Then the two told what had happened along the way to Emmaus, and how they recognized him when he broke the bread.

The same day (it was the first day of the week), at evening, they were still talking about these things. The doors were shut where the disciples were gathered, because they were afraid of the Jewish leaders. But Jesus came in, stood among them, and said, "Peace to you." They were terrified,

Eating Fish and Honey *in Jerusalem*

Luke 24:36-43
John 20:19-23

and thought they had seen a ghost. He said to them, "Why are you troubled? Why do you doubt? Look at my hands and feet. It is I. Touch me, and see. A ghost does not have flesh and bones like I do."

He said this, and showed them his hands and his feet. They could hardly believe it, they were so happy and amazed. So he said, "Do you have any food?" They gave him a piece of a broiled fish and a honeycomb. He took it, and as they watched, he ate it.

Then Jesus said again to them, "Peace to you. Just as my Father sent me, so I send you." He said this, breathed on them, and then said, "Receive the Holy Spirit. If you forgive a person's sins, he is forgiven. But if you refuse to forgive them, the sins remain."

Proving His
Resurrection

Mark 16:14
John 20:24-31

But one of the disciples, Thomas (who was called Didymus), was not there when Jesus came into the locked room. The other disciples told him, "We have seen the Lord." But he said, "Unless I see the wounds caused by the nails in his hands, and actually touch them, I will not believe."

Eight days later, the disciples were again in the room together. Thomas was with them. The doors were shut, but Jesus came in, stood among them, and said, "Peace to you." Then he said to Thomas, "Reach out and touch my hands. Reach here and thrust your hand into my side. Do not be faithless. Believe."

Thomas said to him, "My Lord and my God!" Jesus said, "Thomas, you believe because you have seen me. Those who have not seen me and believe anyway—they are blessed."

He did many other miraculous signs in the presence of his disciples, which are not written in this book. But these are written here so that you can believe that Jesus is the Christ, the Son of God; and that by believing in him you can have eternal life.

After this, Jesus appeared to the disciples again at the Sea of Galilee. Here is how it happened: Simon Peter, Thomas (called Didymus), Nathanael of Cana in Galilee, the sons of Zebedee, and two other disciples were together. Simon Peter said, "I'm going fishing." The others said, "We'll go

Serving Breakfast *at the Sea of Galilee*

John 21:1-14

with you." They went out and boarded a boat, but caught nothing all that night.

When morning came, Jesus stood on the shore, but the disciples didn't know that it was Jesus. He said to them, "Children, do you have any food?" They answered, "No." He said, "Cast the net on the right side of the boat, and you will find fish." They cast the net there, and were not able to draw it back into the boat because there were so many fish in it.

The one whom Jesus loved said to Peter, "It is the Lord." When Simon Peter heard that it was the Lord, he put on his fisherman's coat (for he was dressed down for work), and jumped into the sea. The other disciples came ashore in a little boat (they were not far from land—about three hundred feet), dragging the net full of fish.

As soon as they were ashore, they saw a fire of coals with fish roasting on it, and there was bread. Jesus said to them, "Bring the fish you have caught." Simon Peter drew the net to land. It was full of one hundred and fifty-three big fish. But the net did not break. Jesus said to them,

"Come and dine." And none of the disciples dared ask, "Who are you?" They knew it was the Lord.

Jesus took the bread and fish and gave it to them. This was the third time that Jesus had appeared to his disciples after he had risen from the dead.

So when they had dined, Jesus said to Simon Peter, "Simon, son of John, do you love me more than these?" Peter said to him, "Yes, Lord. You know that I love you." Jesus said to him, "Feed my lambs." Then he said to him the second time, "Simon, son of John, do you love me?" He said to him, "Yes, Lord. You know that I love you." Jesus said to him, "Feed my sheep." And he said to him a third time, "Simon, son of John, do you love me?" Peter was grieved because he asked him for the third time, "Do you love me?" And so he said, "Lord, you know all things. You know that I love you." Jesus said to him, "Feed my sheep.

"Here is the truth: When you were young, you dressed yourself, and went wherever you wanted to go. But when you

Caring for Peter

John 21:15-25

are old, you will allow someone else to dress you, and take you where you don't want to go."

He said this indicating the way Peter would die to glorify God. Then he said to him, "Follow me." Peter looked around and saw the disciple whom Jesus loved following them. This disciple had leaned over to Jesus at the table and asked, "Lord, who will betray you?"

Peter said to Jesus, "Lord, what will this man do?" Jesus said to him, "If I want him to live until I return, what business is that of yours? You follow me." Afterwards the believers thought that Jesus had said that this disciple would not die. But Jesus didn't say, "He won't die." He said, "If I want him to live until I return, what business is that of yours?"

This is the disciple who witnessed these things and has written about them here; and we all know that his report is true. But Jesus did so many other things that, if they were written down, the world could not contain all the books.

The eleven disciples went to the mountain in Galilee as Jesus had instructed. There they saw him and worshipped him. But still some doubted.

Jesus spoke to them: "All the authority in heaven and on earth has been given to me. So, go and make disciples in all the nations; baptize them in the name of the Father, and of the Son, and of the Holy Spirit;teach them to follow all the commands I have given you. And, mind this: I am always with you, even to the end of the age."

Commissioning the Disciples
at Galilee

Matt. 28:16-20
Mark 16:15-18

Then he said, "When I was with you before, I said that all the things written about me in the law of Moses, in the prophets, and in the Psalms, would come true." Then he helped them to understand all these portions of Scripture.

Jesus said to them, "Long ago it was written that Christ would suffer and rise from the dead on the third day. Then, on his authority, repentance and forgiveness of sins would be preached, starting from Jerusalem and extending to all the nations. You are witnesses of these things.

Ascending into Heaven
in Bethany

Mark 16:19-20
Luke 24:44-53

"I will send my Father's promise to you—wait in the city of Jerusalem until you are clothed with power from above." Then he led them to Bethany, lifted up his hands, and blessed them. While he blessed them, he left them, and was taken into heaven. They worshipped him, returned to Jerusalem with great joy, and were constantly in the temple, praising God.

APPENDIX

AN OUTLINE OF THE LIFE OF JESUS CHRIST

CHAPTER ONE—HIS THIRTY YEARS OF PRIVATE LIFE

I.   Introduction—Luke 1:1-4

II. The Genealogies of Jesus Christ
   A. His Jewish Origins—Matt. 1:1–17
   B. His Human Origins—Luke 3:23–38
   C. His Origin as God—John 1:1–18

III. His Birth
   A. John's Birth Is Promised (Jerusalem, c. 7 B.C.)—
      Luke 1:5–25
   B. Gabriel Visits Mary (Nazareth, c. 6 B.C.)—
      Luke 1:26–38
   C. Mary Visits Elizabeth (the Judean Hills)—
      Luke 1:39–56
   D. John Is Born (the Judean Hills)—Luke 1:57–80

E. An Angel Visits Joseph (Nazareth)—Matt. 1:18–25

F. He is Born (Bethlehem, c. 6 B.C.)—Luke 2:1–7

G. Angels Visit the Shepherds (near Bethlehem)—Luke 2:8–20

IV. His Early Life

A. He Is Circumcised (Bethlehem)—Luke 2:21

B. He Is Presented to God (Jerusalem)—Luke 2:22–39

C. The Wise Men Arrive (Jerusalem and Bethlehem, c. 4 B.C.)—Matt. 2:1–12

D. He Escapes to Egypt (from Nazareth)—Matt. 2:13–18

E. He Returns from Egypt (to Nazareth)—Matt. 2:19–23; Luke 2:40

F. He Visits Jerusalem (c. A.D. 9)—Luke 2:41–50

V. He Grows to Manhood (Nazareth)—Luke 2:51–52

CHAPTER TWO—THE BEGINNING OF THE GOSPEL

I. Groundwork for Christ's Ministry

A. John Prepares the Way (Judea, c. A.D. 27)—Luke 3:1–18; Matt. 3:1–12; Mark 1:1–8

B. John Baptizes Jesus (Jordan River)—Luke 3:21–23; Matt. 3:13–17; Mark 1:9–11

C. The Devil Entices Jesus (Judea)—Luke 4:1–13; Matt. 4:1–11; Mark 1:12–13

D. John's Account of Jesus (Bethabara)—John

XV. Prophesying of Persecution—Matt. 10:16–11:1
XVI. Retreating to a Deserted Place
    A. The Death of John—Matt. 14:1–12; Mark 6:14–29; Luke 9:7–9
    B. Feeding Five Thousand (Bethsaida)—Matt. 14:13–23; Mark 6:30–44; Luke 9:10–17; John 6:1–15
    C. Rescuing the Disciples (Sea of Galilee)—Matt. 14:22–36; Mark 6:45–56; John 6:16–21;
XVII. Revealing the Bread of Life
    A. True Bread vs. Miracles (Capernaum)—John 6:22–40
    B. How to Have an Inner Life—John 6:41–59
    C. It Is the Spirit That Gives Life—John 6:60–71
    D. Solving the Problem of Handwashing—Matt. 15:1–20; Mark 7:1–22

CHAPTER FIVE—THE END OF HIS WORK IN GALILEE
I. Retreating Northward
    A. Crumbs for Gentile Dogs (Tyre)—Matt. 15:21–28; Mark 7:24–30
    B. The Astonishment of Decapolis (Decapolis)—Matt. 15:29–31; Mark 7:31–37
II. Visiting Galilee
    A. Feeding Four Thousand (Decapolis)—Matt. 15:32–38; Mark 8:1–9

B. The Leaven of Religious Doctrine (Magdala)
Matt. 15:39–16:12; Mark 8:10–21

C. His Healing Spit (Bethsaida)—Mark 8:22–26

III. Retreating Northward Again

A. The Revelation Which Builds the Church
(Caesarea Philippi)—Matt. 16:13–20; Mark
8:27–30; Luke 9:18–21

B. Predicting His Death and Resurrection—
Matt. 16:21–28; Mark 8:31–9:1;
Luke 9:22–27

C. The Revelation of Jesus Alone (Mt.
Hermon)—Matt. 17:1–13; Mark 9:2–13;
Luke 9:28–36

D. Displaying Faith to a Faithless Generation
(near Mt. Hermon)—Matt. 17:14–20; Mark
9:14–29; Luke 9:37–43

E. Predicting His Death and Resurrection
Again—Matt. 17:22, 23; Mark 9:30–32;
Luke 9:43–45

IV. Returning to Galilee

A. Does God Pay the Temple Tax? (Capernaum)—
Matt. 17:24–27

V. Instructions on the Kingdom

A. Who Is the Greatest?—Matt. 18:1–6; Mark
9:33–42; Luke 9:46–50

B. The Offense of Despising Others—Matt.
18:7–14; Mark 9:43–50

C. How to Care for Others—Matt. 18:15–35

VI. Visiting Jerusalem
   A. The Ridicule of His Family (Capernaum)—
      John 7:1–9
   B. The Marvel of His Teaching (Jerusalem)—
      John 7:10–31
   C. The Religious Leaders Lay a Trap—John
      7:53–8:11
   D. Speaking the Words of His Father—John
      8:12–30
   E. Telling the Liberating Truth—John 8:31–47
   F. Revealing His Eternal Nature—John 8:48–59

CHAPTER SIX—HIS FINAL TRIP TO JERUSALEM
I.   Setting the Standard of Discipleship (on the road
     to Jerusalem)—Matt. 19:1, 2; 8:18–22; Mark
     10:1; Luke 9:51–62
II. Sending Out Seventy Messengers (Galilee and
     Samaria)—Luke 10:1–16
III. Blessing the Seventy—Luke 10:17–24
IV. The Evidence of Eternal Life
     A. Love: The Good Samaritan—Luke 10:25–37
     B. Resting, Not Working: Mary and Martha,
        (Bethany)—Luke 10:38–42
V.   Stopping by Jerusalem
     A. Encountering Spiritual Blindness
        (Jerusalem)—John 9:1–41

B. The Parable of the Shepherd and the Thief—John 10:1–21

C. Retreating from Danger (west of the Jordan River)—John 10:32–42

VI. Describing Life in the Kingdom

A. Praying—The Stone, the Serpent, and the Egg—Luke 11:1–13

B. Hearing the Word of God—The Sign of Jonah—Luke 11:14–32

C. Purity of Heart—The Candle and the Bushel—Luke 11:33–54

D. The Value of Human Life—Luke 12:1–12

E. The Value of Material Possessions—Luke 12:13–21

F. The True Treasure—Luke 12:22–34

G. Responsibility to God—Luke 12:35–48

H. The Kingdom's Conflicts—Luke 12:49–59

I. The Fruit of Repentance—Luke 13:1–9

J. Caring for Others Is Above Keeping the Law—Luke 13:10–17

VII. Describing the Entrance to the Kingdom

A. The Great Tree and the Leavened Bread—Luke 13:18–30

B. "There are last which will be first. . ."—Luke 13:22–35

C. "Whoever exalts himself will be abased. . ."—Luke 14:1–14

D. Invitations to the Kingdom—Luke 14:15–24

CHAPTER SEVEN—THE WEEK OF CHRIST'S DEATH

I. Sunday
   A. The King Rides a Donkey—Matt. 21:1–11;
   B. Mark 11:1–11; Luke 19:28–44; John
      12:12–19

II. Monday
   A. The Fruitless Fig Tree—Matt. 21:18–19
   B. The Wheat Seed's Death—John 12:20–36
   C. Declaring the Focus of Our Faith—John
      12:37–50
   D. The Godless Temple—Matt 21:12–17;
      Mark 11:15–19; Luke 19:45–48

III. Tuesday
   A. The Lesson of the Fig Tree—Matt. 21:20–22;
      Mark 11:20–25
   B. Warning the Religious Leaders
      1. The Parable of Two Sons and a Vineyard—
         Matt. 21:23–32; Mark 11:27–33; Luke
         20:1–8
      2. The Parable of a Son Slain in a Vineyard—
         Matt. 21:33–46; Mark 12:1–12; Luke
         20:9–19
      3. The Parable of the Called and the
         Chosen—Matt. 22:1–14
   C. The Conspiracy Continues
      1. The Pharisees and the Image of Caesar—
         Matt. 22:15–22; Mark 12:13–17; Luke
         20:20–26

IV. Wednesday
  A. The Final Parables (continued)
    1. A Parable About Preparedness—Matt.
       25:1–13
    2. The Parable of Profit—Matt. 25:14–30
    3. The Separation of the Sheep from the
       Goats—Matt. 25:31–46
  B. Judas Joins the Conspiracy—Matt. 26:1–5,
     14–16; Mark 14:1, 2, 10, 11;
     Luke 22:1–6
  C. Peter and John Prepare the Last Meal—Matt.
     26:17–19; Mark 14:12–16; Luke 22:7–13
  D. A Final Gathering
    1. The Footwashing—John 13:1–20
    2. The Betrayer—Matt. 26:20–25; Mark
       14:17–20; Luke 22:21–23; John
       13:21–30
    3. The Lord's Table—Matt. 26:26–29; Mark
       14:21–25; Luke 22:14–20
    4. Love and Denial—Luke 22:31–38; John
       13:33–38
  E. The Final Teaching
    1. The Way to the Father—John 14:1–14
    2. The Coming of the Spirit—Matt. 26:30;
       John 14:15–31
V. Thursday
  A. The Final Teaching (continued)

ABOUT THE AUTHOR

Daniel Partner lives in northern Vermont. He has authored, compiled, and edited many books on topics of interest to Christians. His most recent work includes *The One Year Book of Poetry, Women of Sacred Song—Meditations on Hymns by Women,* and *A Cloud of Witnesses: Fifty Readings on Women of Faith.*

Inspirational Library

Beautiful purse/pocket-size editions of Christian classics bound in flexible leatherette. These books make thoughtful gifts for everyone on your list, including yourself!

When I'm on My Knees The highly popular collection of devotional thoughts on prayer, especially for women.
Flexible Leatherette. $4.97

The Bible Promise Book Over 1,000 promises from God's Word arranged by topic. What does God promise about matters like: Anger, Illness, Jealousy, Love, Money, Old Age, and Mercy? Find out in this book!
Flexible Leatherette. $3.97

Daily Wisdom for Women A daily devotional for women seeking biblical wisdom to apply to their lives. Scripture taken from the New American Standard Version of the Bible.
Flexible Leatherette. $4.97

My Daily Prayer Journal Each page is dated and features a Scripture verse and ample room for you to record your thoughts, prayers, and praises. One page for each day of the year.
Flexible Leatherette. $4.97

Available wherever books are sold.
Or order from:

Barbour Publishing, Inc.
P.O. Box 719
Uhrichsville, OH 44683
http://www.barbourbooks.com

If you order by mail, add $2.00 to your order for shipping.
Prices are subject to change without notice.